D0538563

02   03
—   —
1   1

GAYLORD MG

THE WAY
PEOPLE
LIVE

Life on the Pony Express

THE WAY
PEOPLE
LIVE

Life on the Pony Express

by
Diane Yancey

Lucent Books, P.O. Box 289011, San Diego, CA 92198-9011

Library of Congress Cataloging-in-Publication Data

Yancey, Diane.
    Life on the Pony Express / by Diane Yancey.
        p. cm. — (The way people live)
Includes bibliographical references and index.
    ISBN 1-56006-793-4   7-02   j383.14309
    1. Pony express—Juvenile literature. [1. Pony express.] I. Title. II. Series.
    HE6375.P65 Y36 2001
    383'.143'0973—dc21

00-011643

Contents

Discovering the Humanity in Us All

Books in The Way People Live series focus on groups of people in a wide variety of circumstances, settings, and time periods. Some books focus on different cultural groups, others, on people in a particular historical time period, while others cover people involved in a specific event. Each book emphasizes the daily routines, personal and historical struggles, and achievements of people from all walks of life.

To really understand any culture, it is necessary to strip the mind of the common notions we hold about groups of people. These stereotypes are the archenemies of learning. It does not even matter whether the stereotypes are positive or negative; they are confining and tight. Removing them is a challenge that's not easily met, as anyone who has ever tried it will admit. Ideas that do not fit into the templates we create are unwelcome visitors—ones we would prefer remain quietly in a corner or forgotten room.

The cowboy of the Old West is a good example of such confining roles. The cowboy was courageous, yet soft-spoken. His time (it is always a he, in our template) was spent alternatively saving a rancher's daughter from certain death on a runaway stagecoach, or shooting it out with rustlers. At times, of course, he was likely to get a little crazy in town after a trail drive, but for the most part, he was the epitome of inner strength. It is disconcerting to find out that the cowboy is human, even a bit childish. Can it really be true that cowboys would line up to help the cook on the trail drive grind coffee, just hoping he would give them a little stick of peppermint candy that came with the coffee shipment? The idea of tough cowboys vying with one another to help "Coosie" (as they called their cooks) for a bit of candy seems silly and out of place.

So is the vision of Eskimos playing video games and watching MTV, living in prefab housing in the Arctic. It just does not fit with what "Eskimo" means. We are far more comfortable with snow igloos and whale blubber, harpoons and kayaks.

Although the cultures dealt with in Lucent's The Way People Live series are often historically and socially well-known, the emphasis is on the personal aspects of life. Groups of people, while unquestionably affected by their politics and their governmental structures, are more than those institutions. How do people in a particular time and place educate their children? What do they eat? And how do they build their houses? What kinds of work do they do? What kinds of games do they enjoy? The answers to these questions bring these cultures to life. People's lives are revealed in the particulars and only by knowing the particulars can we understand these cultures' will to survive and their moments of weakness and greatness.

This is not to say that understanding politics does not help to understand a culture. There is no question that the Warsaw ghetto, for example, was a culture that was brought about by the politics and social ideas of Adolf

Hitler and the Third Reich. But the Jews who were crowded together in the ghetto cannot be understood by the Reich's politics. Their life was a day-to-day battle for existence, and the creativity and methods they used to prolong their lives is a vital story of human perseverance that would be denied by focusing only on the institutions of Hitler's Germany. Knowing that children as young as five or six outwitted Nazi guards on a daily basis, that Jewish policemen helped the Germans control the ghetto, that children attended secret schools in the ghetto and even earned diplomas—these are the things that reveal the fabric of life, that can inspire, intrigue, and amaze.

Books in The Way People Live series allow both the casual reader and the student to see humans as victims, heroes, and onlookers. And although humans act in ways that can fill us with feelings of sorrow and revulsion, it is important to remember that "hero," "predator," and "victim" are dangerous terms. Heaping undue pity or praise on people reduces them to objects, and strips them of their humanity.

Seeing the Jews of Warsaw only as victims is to deny their humanity. Seeing them only as they appear in surviving photos, staring at the camera with infinite sadness, is limiting, both to them and to those who want to understand them. To an object of pity, the only appropriate response becomes "Those poor creatures!" and that reduces both the quality of their struggle and the depth of their despair. No one is served by such two-dimensional views of people and their cultures.

With this in mind, The Way People Live series strives to flesh out the traditional, two-dimensional views of people in various cultures and historical circumstances. Using a wide variety of primary quotations—the words not only of the politicians and government leaders, but of the real people whose lives are being examined—each book in the series attempts to show an honest and complete picture of a culture removed from our own by time or space.

By examining cultures in this way, the reader will notice not only the glaring differences from his or her own culture, but also will be struck by the similarities. For indeed, people share common needs—warmth, good company, stability, and affirmation from others. Ultimately, seeing how people really live, or have lived, can only enrich our understanding of ourselves.

An Adventurous Generation

The young men who rode for the Pony Express embodied the adventurous spirit that characterized the United States in the 1850s and '60s. Americans were restless, daring, and willing to risk their safety and comfort in a quest for a better life. The civilized East still pleased some, but thousands more moved westward to satisfy their hunger for open spaces, independence, and prosperity.

Pony Express couriers who raced to and fro across the country between the Missouri River and the Pacific Ocean captured the public's admiration as they expressed its restlessness and daring. Their popularity can be judged by the numerous stories and anecdotes—true accounts, exaggerated reports, and even tall tales—that chronicle their adventures. Today, sorting fact from fiction is often impossible. There is no doubt, however, that these young men were seen as heroes, representing all that was romantic and colorful on the frontier. Western historian Arthur Chapman observes, "Nothing ever attracted more attention to the West. The rawest tenderfoot who turned westward knew there was a Pony Express and would have been disappointed if he had not seen a rider."[1]

The riders were more than popular heroes, however. They were some of the first national postmen, and their services helped relieve the loneliness that was a fact of life for thousands of prospectors and pioneers who had left friends and family behind when they moved west. The draw of gold in California and Colorado was a powerful magnet to many Americans, but most found that living in distant places produced an ache of homesickness that only a letter or a package from home could ease.

Gold!

The acquisition of the Oregon Territory and the Republic of California by the United States in 1848 offered many opportunities for settlement and a fresh start in the West. Gold was discovered in California that year as well, and thousands of adventurers streamed westward in the hopes of "striking it rich" on the new frontier.

The gold rush began near Sacramento, when James W. Marshall picked up a handful of nuggets out of the American River and recognized their worth. One of the young men working with Marshall later remembered: "Marshall went alone into the tailrace [the water channel for floating away mine tailings and refuse]. In a few minutes he came back with a most pleasant smile on his face, carrying his old white hat in his arms, saying, 'Boys . . . I believe I have found a gold mine.'"[2]

Marshall tried to keep the discovery quiet, but it was a vain hope, and a local rush to find gold began. Sailors in San Francisco heard the news and jumped ship. Blacksmiths left their forges. Farmers tossed aside their plows, and

California became part of the United States in 1848, the same year that gold was discovered there.

clerks put down their pens in the hurry to find riches. Due to poor mail service, word of the great discovery trickled slowly back to the East and took six months to make an impact, but then the news sparked a migration that was unmatched in U.S. history.

The thousands who flooded into the West beginning in 1849 soon discovered that they were virtually out of touch with friends and family in the East. Travel across the country was a slow, dangerous business, and visits back and forth with loved ones were all but impossible. Mail was erratic, and news of the nation was always several months old by the time it reached California. An 1851 report from the postmaster general summed up the situation in a few words: "The mail service in California and Oregon has been so irregular in its performance . . . that it is not included in this statement."[3]

Mounted Mailmen

When mail arrived in the West, it often did not reach the addressee because many men never went to town to pick it up. In 1851 the postmaster general reported that twenty-four hundred pounds of unclaimed mail had accumulated in California.

Recognizing a problem, and the fact that they could make more money carrying mail to

As America's expansion continued westward, the need for fast, reliable cross-country mail service became a necessity.

the gold camps than mining for the precious metal, a few enterprising individuals decided to collect the mail in towns like San Francisco, Sacramento, and Placerville, and transport it by horse and pack mule to miners in the hills.

Alexander H. Todd was one of the first of these individuals, a young gold hunter who discovered that his health was not strong enough for work in the "diggings." Todd had himself sworn in as a postal clerk, charged $1 each to register miners who expected to get mail regularly, then carried letters and packages to the camps. In pay, he received up to an ounce of gold dust ($16) for each item he delivered.

Other private entrepreneurs, insightful men who recognized a need, soon acknowledged Todd's good sense and started similar express companies throughout the Mother Lode (the gold-bearing region of the California foothills running through present-day Mariposa, Tuolumne, Calaveras, Amador, El Dorado, Placer, and Nevada Counties.) With competition, prices soon dropped to reasonable levels, but many men were still able to make a good living at their newfound occupation.

The appearance of mounted mailmen in the gold camps became cause for great celebration among homesick, isolated prospectors. In his *Penknife Sketches*, writer and prospector

Alonzo Delano describes events upon the arrival of the mail to a local general store:

> Every pick and shovel is dropped, every pan is laid aside, every rocker is stopped with its half-washed dirt, every claim is deserted, and they crowd around the store with eager inquiries, "Have you got a letter for me?"
>
> With what joy it is seized, and they care little whether they pay two or five dollars for it, they've got a letter. Or perhaps as is often the case, the answer is "There's nothing for you," and with a "Damn the luck" and a heavy heart, they go sullenly back to work, unfitted by disappointment for social intercourse for the rest of the day.[4]

Bold, Bright Young Fellows

Pony Express services in western gold camps were less organized than the national counterpart later established by William Russell. Joaquin Miller, who worked in the gold fields, described these small business enterprises and the young men who operated them in Arthur Chapman's book *The Pony Express.*

"The Pony Express was a great feature in the gold mines of California long before anyone ever thought of putting it on the plains. Every creek, camp or 'city' had its Pony Express which ran to and from the nearest office. At Yreka we had the Humbug Creek Express, the Deadwood Camp Express, the Greenhorn, and so on.

The rider was always a bold, bright young fellow, who owned the line, horses and all, and had his 'office' in some responsible store. He crowded an immense deal of personality into his work; would die in the saddle rather than delay ten minutes over the expected time. He was, of course, always a dashing rider, dressed gayly [*sic*] and blew a small bugle as he went up and down the creek at a plunging rate. 'Three blasts, after the fashion of the London postman!' Whack and bang at the cabin door meant a letter for this or that 'claim,' as the rider dashed down the trail under the trees. . . . Away, over the boulders with a bound, with pay for the letter clutched in his fist! He grabs the letter, away bounds the spirited pony, another blast of the horn!"

Mail by Sea

Just as regional mail service in the 1850s was haphazard throughout the West, mail service from the East to the West was unreliable as well. Some Americans simply entrusted a letter to a friend or even a stranger who was traveling across country and who accepted responsibility for getting it to its owner at the other end of the line. Some of these missives were successfully delivered in time; others were lost or forgotten.

Mail delivery was traditionally a government obligation, however, and Congress was in charge of ensuring that an official means of transporting mail existed. In carrying out this responsibility, it decided on a favorable route and determined the amount of financial compensation that would be paid to a private contractor who would perform the work. Except for a generous payment to shipping lines that carried the bulk of the mail to California, most of these subsidies were extremely low, sometimes less than $20,000 a year. If a contractor failed to live up to his obligations, his contract could be canceled. If his costs were more than his receipts, he could petition Congress for more money (usually unsuccessfully) or absorb his losses, often at the price of going out of business.

The first and foremost mail routes to and from California were sea routes. Most mail was transported on a monthly or semimonthly schedule "Round the Horn" (New York to San Francisco via Cape Horn) or by the "Isthmus Route"—to Panama, where it was loaded onto railroad cars and conveyed through disease-infested jungles, then reloaded onto a ship and carried north to appropriate ports. Even the shorter route totaled six thousand miles and could take a month or more to complete.

Sometimes a ship was waylaid by storms. Sometimes it was slowed by problems with the crew. Mail delivery by sea was more reliable than by land, however, and companies such as the United States Mail Steamship Company and the Pacific Mail Steamship Line were able to charge extremely high rates for their services because they had virtually no competition.

The Oxbow Route

Because sea routes were expensive, slow, and uncertain, Congress also considered proposals to carry mail across overland routes. In 1850 Samuel H. Woodson of Missouri won the first contract to carry mail by wagon and pack mule between Independence, Missouri, and Salt Lake City, Utah. Due to poor planning, his deliveries were irregular in summer and almost nonexistent in winter, and he went out of business within four years.

In 1851 Absalom Woodward and George Chorpenning Jr. won a government contract to carry mail by mule—"Jackass Mail"— between Sacramento and Salt Lake City, a distance of about nine hundred miles. Woodward was killed by members of the Shoshone tribe on one of the first trips, however. Continuing attacks, bad weather, and inadequate funds put an end to Chorpenning's endeavors about 1859.

In 1857 John Butterfield's Overland Mail Company was awarded government funding of $600,000 annually and became the most efficient means of transporting mail across the continent. Butterfield, a practical and experienced stage operator, built 139 stations (rest stops), constructed new roads and bridges, and improved existing ones along a southern "oxbow" (U-shape) route that began in both Memphis, Tennessee, and St. Louis, Missouri, united near Fort Smith, Arkansas, then ran through Texas and what would become Arizona before it looped north to San Francisco. The length of the run was a record 2,795 miles.

Butterfield's stages ran twice a week and accommodated passengers plus several hundred pounds of letters and newspapers. The route was rough and hazardous, however. Marauding Apaches and Comanches roamed the desert plains, and the summer's heat caused one passenger to remark that he had been "as close to hell as he ever wished to be."[5]

To compensate for the length of the route, Butterfield strove for swiftness and punctuality. His runs covered nearly three thousand miles in twenty-five days or less, a grueling schedule that kept drivers under constant pressure. He cautioned, "Every person in the Company's employ will remember that each minute is of importance. If each driver on the route loses 15 minutes, it would make a total loss of time, on the entire route, of 25 hours, or, more than one day."[6] Due to his insistence and expertise, the Butterfield stages ran on schedule for more than two years, an outstanding performance for an early-day transportation company.

An Overland Route

In the 1850s, well established sea routes seemed quicker and less risky than overland mail routes. Nevertheless, they were tremendously expensive. Thus, the fight for reliable mail service across the central United States continued, despite the following drawbacks, as detailed in Howard R. Driggs's *The Pony Express Goes Through.*

"Along the line between Salt Lake City and Independence, Missouri, serious difficulties were . . . being experienced by the stalwarts that were trying to get the mail through. The Indians did not give so much trouble on that part of the Central Route in the early fifties; but the heavy snows and the mud did. One of the mail-carriers was frozen to death on the trail; others were severely frostbitten; some of them were nearly starved at times before they could reach the widely scattered supply-stations. It was an almost superhuman task to battle through the blizzards that swept over the plains and high mountains. A mail line along the shorter route seemed utterly out of the question.

Nor was all clear sailing on the more southern route. Though mud and snow gave little trouble there, the Indians did. Attacks on the mail became more frequent. After several carriers had been killed and their letters scattered to the winds, the postmaster in Salt Lake sent out a notice advising business men to duplicate their important correspondence, doubly to assure themselves against loss of such mail along the dangerous and uncertain overland lines."

Politics and the Mail

By the end of 1858, four privately owned overland mail routes were operating across the nation including a monthly mail/passenger service from Kansas City, Missouri, to Stockton, California; a semiweekly passenger and mail service from San Antonio, Texas, to San Diego; a weekly mail/passenger service from Missouri to California operated jointly by John M. Hockaday and George Chorpenning; and Butterfield's Overland Mail Company. The latter was certainly the most famous and heavily patronized of the four.

Butterfield stages departed twice a week and were remarkably reliable, but they did not satisfy many Californians, who believed that a shorter mail route could be established. The most obvious would be one that ran across the central part of the country, following the Oregon–California Trail, which stretched from Independence, Missouri, to the West Coast. Thousands of pioneers followed this trail in the 1850s, and freight caravans hauling supplies to U.S. Army posts ran along it regularly. Discoveries of gold in Colorado in 1858 and silver in Nevada in 1859 meant that more people were settling in these central regions as well, with an accompanying demand for reliable and rapid mail service.

Politics, however, blocked any significant government support for a central mail route. The United States was strongly divided by the issues of slavery and states' rights by the late 1850s, and Postmaster General Aaron V. Brown was a southerner. He naturally supported Butterfield's southern route rather than a more northerly one, as did southern congressmen, who wanted to control the mail to California if secession from the Union became a reality.

Then, in March 1859, Brown suddenly died and was succeeded by Joseph Holt. Holt decided to reduce the expenses of the post office and slashed support for all overland routes except Butterfield's. Services were cut or shut down and contracts went unrenewed. Soon, cash-strapped companies such as Hockaday's were out of business or on the verge of bankruptcy.

A Dream Becomes Reality

Such was the state of the country in 1860 when visionary businessman William H. Russell opted to risk his fortune and reputation in establishing an express mail service across the central part of the country. The Pony Express was a private institution, independent of the government, and it existed only from April

A nineteenth-century newspaper advertises passenger and mail service across the continental United States.

Swift Couriers

The Pony Express is an integral part of postal history, a service that helped advance the development of the West. Writer Arthur King Peters gives a thumbnail sketch of this legendary episode in American history in his book, *Seven Trails West*.

"'Neither rain nor snow nor heat of day nor gloom of night shall stay these couriers from the swift fulfillment of their appointed rounds.' The Pony Express performance seems to personify this inscription above the portico of the main post office building in New York City, yet surprisingly the Pony Express was never an official part of the U.S. Postal Service. It was a private mail system, a hell-for-leather bucket brigade on horseback—instead of water, the young Pony Express riders hauled saddlebags stuffed with mail. Riding night and day around the clock, the unbroken chain of Pony Express couriers delivered its mail nearly two thousand miles, between Saint Joseph, Missouri, and San Francisco, California, in only ten days. Never before in human history had written communication been moved so swiftly, over such distances, and with such regularity."

1860 through October 1861—a total of nineteen months. (Some historians count only eighteen months because mail service was interrupted for about four weeks during the Paiute War.)

Still, the service captured the public's imagination and support, and, in the words of another postmaster general, Arthur E. Summerfield, "left a deep and inspiring mark in the annals of American adventure."[7] Due to the commitment of its riders, it was more effective than anyone could have foreseen and paved the way for transportation and communication advancements of later decades. Chapman writes:

> The youngsters who took so gayly [*sic*] to such an unheard-of task must have amazed even the dreamer, Russell, whom the world has to thank for a "failure" so glorious that it will be remembered forever. The riders of the Pony Express made that institution greater in reality than it could have been in the fondest imaginings of the romanticist who planned it.[8]

The Bright Idea

The Pony Express was considered a novel and bold scheme when it was first revealed to the public in the spring of 1860. In fact, however, the notion of a horse relay system to carry mail was not as unique as it sounded. The concept was an ancient one, dating back to Europe and Asia in the first century and beyond.

The Pony Express's Predecessors

Darius the Great, ruler of Persia from 522 to 486 B.C., was the first to establish a highly efficient communication system using horses to carry messages and mail across the country. So excellent was Darius's system that the royal mail was transported fifteen hundred miles between the capital of Susa to the town of Sardis in ten days. It could take an ordinary traveler three months to cover the same distance.

Roman emperor Augustus (27 B.C.–14 A.D.) patterned his horse relay system on that of Darius's, again using it only to carry royal mail. On main highways, fresh horses were stabled in stations ten miles apart, and messengers ordinarily covered about one hundred miles a day. Riders who carried the news of Emperor Nero's death to his successor, however, rode 332 miles in thirty-six hours.

The most impressive horse relay system in history was established by Kublai Khan, emperor of China from about 1279 to 1294 A.D. Explorer Marco Polo describes elaborate

stations set up along mail roads to house weary travelers as well as stable horses that were used to carry messages. Four hundred horses were kept in readiness at each station, even in mountainous regions off the main roads. At least two hundred thousand horses were used in the Khan's relay system, and ten thousand buildings were maintained.

Augustus Caesar used a horse relay system to carry royal mail.

Polo writes that messengers for the Khan bound their bodies and heads tightly with cloths to minimize injury from the long rides they endured and mentions that in this way (and because of the excellence of their horses) they were able to accomplish up to 250 miles a day. "In cases of great emergency they continue their course during the night, and if there should be no moon, they are accompanied to the next station by persons on foot, who run before them with lights,"[9] he notes.

Ancient rulers were not the only men to establish pony express systems, however. In the 1750s, Deputy Postmaster General Benjamin Franklin used a horse courier system to provide speedy domestic mail service in the American colonies. In 1825 journalist David Hale used horse relays to collect news around the state of New York, and in 1830 Richard Haughton, editor of the *New York Journal of Commerce* and later the *Boston Atlas*, used a similar system to collect returns from every town in Massachusetts the morning following an election. James Watson Webb of the *New York Courier and Enquirer* set up a pony express between New York and Washington, D.C., in 1832. On the West Coast, in 1847 General Stephen W. Kearny, military governor of California, established a horse courier service made up of two soldiers who met twice monthly and exchanged letters and official communications halfway between San Diego and San Francisco.

The Originators

No one can say with certainty who first conceived the idea of a nationwide pony express in the United States in the 1850s. The demands for improved mail service were so pressing, and the idea of using horses to expedite schedules was so logical, that the notion seemed to spring up in several places at about the same time.

Senator William M. Gwin of California and Benjamin Ficklin, who became one of the managers of the Pony Express in 1860, appear to be the earliest to suggest the idea of a weekly mail express across the United States. The two men met on a journey from San Francisco to Washington, D.C., in 1854, at which time they talked about the possibility of creating a pony express service on a central route.

Shortly after that trip, Gwin, a member of the Senate Committee on Post Offices and Post Roads, introduced a bill intended to establish weekly mail service between St. Louis, Missouri, and San Francisco, California. The bill—calling for a $1 million military road to be built to California, five military forts to offer protection, and a soldier guard to accompany the mail along the most dangerous parts of the route—died in committee. However, when the Pony Express was formed in 1860, Gwin claimed credit for himself and Ficklin. He later wrote in his *Memoirs*, (which were written in third-person point of view):

On the 18th of January (1855), Mr. Gwin introduced a bill in the Senate to establish an express weekly mail between St. Louis, Mo., and San Francisco but did not succeed in getting it enacted into a law, but the enterprising mail contractor [William Russell] on the central route through Salt Lake established, at his own expense, and his own risk, this weekly mail, known as the pony express, which through the energy of Mr. B. F. Ficklin, who originated the scheme and carried it into operation, became a great success.[10]

Californian Frederick A. Bee, who built the first telegraph line across the Sierra

As U.S. deputy postmaster, Benjamin Franklin provided prompt mail service to the American colonies using a horse courier service.

Nevada mountains, is another possible originator of the pony express idea. In 1859 Bee tried to raise support for a horse relay that would carry telegrams between the Sierra Nevadas and the Missouri River. Bee claimed to have shared his idea with William Russell in the fall of 1859 and reportedly argued for the plan before the Senate Committee on Post Offices and Post Roads in an attempt to win government support for Russell's mail service on the central route.

John Scudder, an employee of Russell, wrote that he and his fellow workers mapped a proposed route for a horse relay service and sent it to Russell in 1859, just months before the Pony Express was established. Their letter apparently caught Russell's interest, because it brought a request for more details.

John Butterfield of the Overland Mail Company appears to have conceived of a pony relay service as well. An article in a San Francisco newspaper on March 23, 1860, stated,

> The announcement of Russell, Majors and Co., the well known contractors on the Salt Lake route, that they intend in April to start a Horse Express to Placerville, via the Great Salt Lake, has caused a fluttering among the friends of the Butterfield route. It appears the scheme originated with Mr. Butterfield himself in this city about three months ago.[11]

Butterfield apparently shelved his own horse relay plans when William Russell announced the Pony Express in early 1860.

As the founder of the Pony Express, William Russell is not often given credit for originating the idea himself, but such could have been the case. Charles R. Morehead Jr., one of Russell's employees, states in his *Personal Recollections* that Russell came up with the idea and discussed it with Secretary of War John B. Floyd in Morehead's presence in Washington early in 1858. "While the Pony Express was conceived at that time by Mr. Russell . . . ," Morehead writes, "it was not put into operation by him and his associates until 1860."[12]

The Partners

With so many men claiming to have proposed the service, the idea for the Pony Express probably came to William Russell from several different people over a period of months or years. Indisputably, he was the founder and prime mover of the venture that became a well-known chapter in U.S. history.

Russell seemed a logical person to put the Pony Express experiment to the test. An opportunist with an eye for the future, he had financial ability, was a fearless risk taker, and had plenty of optimism and self-confidence. In his mid-thirties he became involved in the freighting business. By 1855, at the age of forty-three, he had become a wealthy and influential man, president of the mammoth freighting firm Russell, Majors & Waddell, headquartered in Leavenworth, Kansas Territory. There he built a fine reputation and was admired by many as one of the foremost freighters of the time, a veritable "Napoleon of the West."[13] Some contemporaries, however, characterized him differently, as an "incorrigible, wheeler and dealer."[14]

Much of the freight Russell handled traveled along a central route to army posts out

John Butterfield's Overland Mail Company stages (pictured) faced many hazards as they followed the Oxbow Route. Butterfield was one of many who dreamed of a Pony Express.

west. He was not a frontiersman, however, and never experienced life along the trail. Instead, he preferred to leave those business details in the hands of his partner Alexander Majors. Majors, a successful overland freight man even before he teamed up with Russell in 1855, was practical, conscientious, and deeply religious, never allowing his men or his animals to work on Sunday. He often traveled with his supply trains and knew the hardships of life in the West—unpredictable weather, difficult terrain, and hostile Indians. One observer writes, "His outfits were very efficient since he himself had performed every task from driving oxen in searing summer heat and numbing winter cold to cooking under the stars over a campfire of cow-chips."[15]

The firm's third partner, William B. Waddell, took care of finances, inventories, and other office concerns of the great company. A cautious, frugal conservative, Waddell preferred solid investments to speculation and was the opposite of Russell in personality. Author Roy Bloss notes:

> While the enterprising Russell busied himself on prolonged jaunts to New York and Washington . . . and while the intrepid Majors was plodding across the wilderness with an endless line of canopied conestogas [wagons], William B. Waddell stayed at home, the watchdog of the exchequer [treasury] and manager of the day-to-day trivia that required proprietary decision.[16]

Expanding Business Concerns

The firm of Russell, Majors & Waddell was not the limit of William Russell's business undertakings. Always hoping to expand his

sphere of influence, he borrowed money in 1859 and started another business with John S. Jones, a freight man from Missouri. Together, the two men began providing daily stage and mail service between Leavenworth and Denver, Colorado, where gold had been discovered in 1858. The service was called the Leavenworth & Pike's Peak Express Company (L&PP Express). Alexander Majors and William Waddell did not join in the venture, being more cautious than their ambitious associate and unwilling to invest their money in what they saw as a risky venture.

Russell's stage service was popular, but, as Majors and Waddell anticipated, it did not make money. Carrying goods and services on the frontier was extremely expensive, and the public would only tolerate so much when it came to mail and transportation charges. The L&PP Express lost $1,000 a day. When overdue bills had to be paid, Russell turned to his partners to bail out the new business with funds from Russell, Majors & Waddell.

Also in 1859, Russell bought out John M. Hockaday's stage line, which had struggled to carry mail and passengers from Missouri to Salt Lake City since 1858. This expansion allowed Russell to shift his Denver stages to a more central route. It also made it possible for him to think about competing with Butterfield's Overland Mail Company for the government's overland mail contract.

The COC&PP Express

The L&PP Express, expanded by Hockaday's line, was renamed the Central Overland California & Pike's Peak Express Company (COC&PP Express) in May 1860, and the new stage line was upgraded to meet Russell's standards. "I was compelled to build a world-wide reputation, even at considerable

Robbers' Roost in Colorado, was one of the many stations where stage coaches stopped for food and fresh horses.

expense . . . and also to incur large expenses in many ways, the details of which I cannot commit to paper,"[17] he wrote to Waddell in mid-1860.

Hockaday had opted to stop his stagecoaches every few hours to let his animals rest and graze rather than using relays of teams. Russell, however, preferred a relay system in which teams were changed for new ones every few hours and coaches continued almost nonstop down the road. Under such a system, more horses and mules had to be provided and new stations built along the route to house the teams. Each station had to be staffed by a station manager and stocked with supplies for passengers and animals. Such improved quality of service increased the line's efficiency and popularity, but bills (and debts) continued to mount alarmingly.

Optimistic even in the face of adversity, Russell became convinced that a government subsidy for carrying mail would help pull the COC&PP Express out of the red. In the winter of 1859–60, he traveled to Washington,

D.C., where he discussed ways of accomplishing those goals with Senator Gwin. Gwin had already stated his support for a fast overland mail service. Now the two men agreed that the time was right to begin such a flamboyant undertaking. Chapman captures the drama and excitement of their vision when he writes:

> Men and horses were to form a veritable telegraph line of flesh and blood between the muddy Missouri and the bright Pacific. It was to be a super-service of speed, kept going day and night at all seasons of the year and demonstrating that the objections to a northern mail route were based on prejudice or misinformation.[18]

With characteristic enthusiasm, on January 27, 1860, Russell sent a dispatch to his son John W. Russell, secretary of the COC&PP Express. It read: "Have determined to establish a Pony Express to Sacramento, California, commencing 3rd of April. Time ten days."[19]

Managers and Superintendents

Alexander Majors and William Waddell were not happy when they learned of Russell's plan to start a new kind of mail service across the United States. They doubted the wisdom of this latest speculation, especially since the COC&PP Express had not yet proved profitable. Russell, however, argued that if the central route proved faster and more reliable than a southern one, they would get more mail contracts including government funded assignments. As a clinching argument, he stressed that he had given his word to Gwin that he would establish a pony express. Majors and Waddell were high-principled men who believed in honoring commitments, so the two reluctantly agreed to help get the new venture under way.

Russell oversaw some of the setup at the eastern end, and Majors's practical expertise helped in the matter of purchasing livestock and supplies, but the partners were too busy running their existing freight and stage businesses to supervise every detail of the new operation. Instead, they relied on other employees hired for the purpose. William W. Finney, general agent of the Pacific, was in charge of overseeing the company's interests in San Francisco. Route Superintendent Benjamin Ficklin, who had worked for both the L&PP Express and the COC&PP Express, became the operational head of the company for a time.

Five division superintendents were put in charge of sections of the line. A. E. Lewis, stationed in St. Joseph, Missouri, had responsibil-

Murderous Jack Slade

Division superintendent Joseph Slade had a mixed reputation as a murderer and powerful law enforcer in the West. In *The Expressmen*, author David Nevin gives a glimpse of Slade's brutal approach to life, which eventually proved his undoing. He was hung in Virginia City, Montana, in 1864 when his outrageous behavior grew too violent for ordinary citizens to accept.

"The Sweetwater line [a section of trail between Julesburg, Colorado, westward into Wyoming] had one notable asset—the division superintendent, Joseph Alfred ('Captain Jack') Slade. A soft-spoken, short, roly-poly fellow, Slade was in fact a fugitive from a murder charge in Illinois, and the suspected perpetrator of as many as 26 killings in all. . . . Slade imposed so forceful a stewardship that Sweetwater Division coaches steadily improved their record of punctuality and secu-

rity. 'True,' wrote Mark Twain, 'in order to bring about this wholesome change Slade had to kill several men—some say three, others say four and others six—but the world was the richer for their loss.'

One victim was Jules Reni, who had been stationmaster at Julesburg before the Slade era. After Slade reclaimed some stage horses Reni had stolen, Reni caught Slade unarmed one day and emptied a revolver into him. But Slade survived, and after recovering he had Reni hunted down and brought to him by company agents. He lashed his prisoner to a corral post overnight in the cold, then in the morning began using him for target practice. Between pistol shots, Slade gulped whiskey and gleefully told Reni where he was going to hit him next. Reni died with 22 holes in him. Slade cut off his ears and carried them around as souvenirs."

ity from that town to Fort Kearny, Nebraska. Joseph A. Slade managed the line from Fort Kearny to the Horseshoe Station in Wyoming. James E. Bromley oversaw the division between Horseshoe Station and Salt Lake City. Howard Egan's territory ran from Salt Lake City, where he resided, to Roberts Creek Station in Nevada, while Bolivar Roberts oversaw Roberts Creek to Sacramento.

Each of the five was responsible for setting up his division and had to ensure the smooth running of the relay once it was under way, as Chapman explains:

> It was "up to" the division superintendent to see that the livestock was kept in good condition; to apprehend horse thieves; to keep stations supplied when no supplies were in sight; to see that substitutes were available when riders were sick or injured, or had suddenly quit the service; and to build anew on the ruins of stations that had been destroyed by Indians. In addition, they had to supervise the running of the stages and to look after the wants of transcontinental passengers, many of whom were unreasonable in their demands.[20]

The superintendents were brave, capable men who understood the dangers and difficulties of life on their particular section of the route. For instance, Joseph Slade had worked for L&PP Express since 1858 and had singlehandedly cleaned out a band of outlaws that had headquartered at one of the stage stations in his territory. One author observes, "Slade's exploits in cleaning up the stage line gained him such a fearful reputation that his very name was enough to hold criminals in check."[21] Superintendent Howard Egan had been one of the personal bodyguards for Mormon leader Joseph Smith and had accompanied Brigham Young on his journey from Illinois to Utah in search of a home for the Mormons. Egan's son testified:

> He knew the country. He could handle men. He would never ask anyone—rider or station keeper—to do anything he would not do himself. Dangers to him were just part of the job. He obeyed strictly the orders of those above him, and he expected his men to do the same.[22]

The superintendents traveled up and down the trail as conditions warranted, and station attendants had to be reliable and hardworking if they wanted to give satisfaction. According to one writer, "The division superintendents never announced their coming. They might descend from an incoming stage, or they might patrol the trail on horseback. Their word was law, and their law was harsh. Sometimes it had to be backed up with a gun."[23] Despite their reputations for toughness, most superintendents were fair, peaceable men who went above and beyond the call of duty to help make the Pony Express a success.

Preparations

Russell intended for his pony relay to begin on April 3, 1860, so there was much to do in a very short time. As owner of the COC&PP Express, he already had stagecoach stations at his disposal between Missouri and Salt Lake City, but these depots were too far apart for Pony Express purposes. Intermediate ones had to be established. In the unsettled spaces west of Salt Lake City, stations had to be constructed by work crews sent out from Utah and California. When all were completed, about 190 stations dotted the route between St. Joseph and Sacramento.

Station Builders

The following episode, recounted by veteran rider J. G. Kelley, occurred during the Paiute War when a series of stations had to be rebuilt after Indian violence in the desert. The story gives a glimpse of the hardships endured by the men who carved Pony Express stations out of the Nevada wilderness. Kelley's narrative is included in William Lightfoot Visscher's *A Thrilling and Truthful History of the Pony Express*.

"I was a Pony Express rider in 1860, and went out with [division superintendent] Bolivar Roberts, and I tell you it was no picnic. No amount of money could tempt me to repeat my experience of those days. To begin with, we had to build willow roads, corduroy fashion, across many places along the Carson River, carrying bundles of willows two and three hundred yards in our arms, while the mosquitoes were so thick that it was difficult to tell whether the man was white or black, so thickly were they piled on his neck, face, and arms.

Arriving at the Sink of the Carson River, we began the erection of a fort [station] to protect us from the Indians. As there were no rocks or logs in that vicinity, it was built of adobes, made from the mud on the shores of the lake. To mix this and get it to the proper consistency to mould into adobes, we tramped all day in our bare feet. This we did for a week or more, and the mud being strongly impregnated with alkali carbonate of soda, you can imagine the condition of our feet. They were much swollen and resembled hams."

Mail collection points were set up in the East and West and a few points in between. In New York City the office of Jerome B. Simpson, one of Russell's friends and creditors, was the designated dropoff point. In San Francisco William Finney's headquarters at the Alta Telegraph office was the collection site. Other appropriate drop sites were chosen in Washington, D.C., Chicago, St. Louis, Salt Lake City, and other cities.

Deadlines for collection were specified. For instance, an ad in a San Francisco paper read: "Letters will be received at San Francisco until 2 3/4 o'clock P.M. each day of departure. . . . Telegraphic Dispatches will be received at Carson City until 6 o'clock P.M. every Wednesday."[24] The cost of carrying a letter was spelled out as well—$5 per half ounce, with letters carried between San Francisco and Salt Lake City initially costing only $3 per half ounce. Government postage in addition to these carrying charges was about ten cents per letter.

Not only did stations have to be created and charges determined, but riders had to be hired as well. Experienced riders were one of the most vital aspects of the new service, and great effort was made to secure the best and most enthusiastic men. Division superintendents handled this part of the job. Beginning in March, advertisements such as the following, taken from the pages of the *Sacramento Daily Union*, were placed in newspapers along the route:

MEN WANTED! The undersigned wishes to hire ten or a dozen men, familiar with the management of horses, as hostlers, or riders on the Overland Express Route via Salt Lake City. Wages $50 per month. . . .

Another advertisement that circulated in San Francisco was more specific in its requirements and generous in its pay offer: "Wanted—young, skinny, wiry fellows not over 18. Must be expert riders, willing to risk death daily. Orphans preferred. Wages $25 a week."[26] So enthusiastic was the response to such ads that openings were usually filled in one or two days.

While superintendents lined up riders for the job, purchasing agents looked for horses.

Specially made lightweight saddles were designed and ordered. Supplies were shipped across country to the most remote and desolate of the stations. Total expenses were heavy at the outset. Greene Majors, son of Alexander Majors, later summed up the arrangements and outlay:

To establish the Pony Express required five hundred of the best blooded American horses; one hundred and ninety stock stations for changing the riding stock; two hundred station tenders to care for the horses and have them ready, saddles and bridles, for the incoming rider to mount and be off like the wind; eighty of the

Enthusiastic young men eagerly accepted positions with the Pony Express.

keenest, toughest, bravest of western youths for the riders, with stations all supplied with hay, grain, and other needed materials. It required $100,000 in gold coin to establish and equip the line. [27]

Shaky Finances

Russell did not cut corners while putting the Pony Express together, since he had the vast resources and the good credit of Russell, Majors & Waddell upon which to draw. Horace Greeley, founder of the *New York Tribune*, traveled west in 1859 and viewed the company's headquarters in Leavenworth. He describes it thus:

Russell, Majors & Waddell's transportation establishment, between the fort and the city, is the great feature of Leavenworth. Such acres of wagons; such pyramids of extra axle-trees; such herds of oxen; such regiments of drivers and other employees! No one who does not see can realize how vast a business this is; nor how numerous are it outlays as well as its revenue. I presume this great firm has at this hour two millions of dollars invested in stock, mainly oxen, mules and wagons. They last year employed six thousand teamsters and worked forty-five thousand oxen.[28]

Neither Greeley or any other outside observer could have guessed that the huge enterprise would be on the verge of bankruptcy in 1860. Its monetary problems stemmed largely from the army's failure to pay for huge amounts of supplies that had been shipped west in 1857 and 1858. Hoping to make up for that shortfall, Russell had invested in the COC&PP Express, but that proved costly rather than profitable.

Therefore, throughout the entire Pony Express venture, Russell, Majors, and Waddell had to work desperately to keep their

The Visionary

William Hepburn Russell's willingness to take risks brought the Pony Express into existence, but also contributed to his financial downfall. Authors Raymond W. and Mary Lund Settle put his character into perspective in the following excerpt from their book *Saddles and Spurs: The Pony Express Saga*.

"From the very beginning Russell's business career was remarkable for breadth and variety of interests. Always, he was ready to go into anything that showed promise of profit. He has been characterized as 'visionary,' a 'plunger' and even as a 'gambler' by critics whose knowledge of him and the times in which he lived were incomplete and faulty. This is wholly unfair. Speculator he was, on a broad-gauge scale, like every other man on the frontier who had an extra dollar or could borrow one. Land was cheap, the country was filling up with settlers, business was booming, the West was being exploited, and the foundations for fortunes . . . were being laid. The names of a dozen men in Lafayette County and scores of others elsewhere who were his counterparts, could be recorded. Some of them achieved wealth and hung onto it. Others, like Russell, got it only to lose it. If he deserves any of those harsh cognomens [names], so do they all."

businesses afloat, repeatedly borrowing money and stalling creditors. Eventually, in an effort to get money to maintain the shaky enterprises, William Russell became involved in a scheme that involved illegally borrowing Indian Trust Fund bonds with the help of a government employee. The bonds were used as collateral for loans to help keep Russell's businesses from going bankrupt.

Russell was caught and went to prison for a time in December 1860, charged with conspiring to defraud the government. He maintained, however, that he was entitled to the money, since the army owed the Russell, Majors & Waddell firm a huge sum. Eventually his case was dismissed on a technicality. Nevertheless, his financial shortcomings ultimately contributed to the failure of the Pony Express and his personal downfall.

"Great Express Adventure"

As all the pieces of the Pony Express enterprise came together and the starting date drew near, the venture was publicized and promoted to capture the attention of businesses and the public. Russell's son, John W. Russell, had taken responsibility for releasing the first tidings of the new endeavor early in the year. On January 30, 1860, the *Leavenworth Daily Times* carried an article headlined:

> GREAT EXPRESS ADVENTURE FROM LEAVENWORTH TO SACRAMENTO IN TEN DAYS. CLEAR THE TRACK AND LET THE PONY COME THROUGH.[29]

In March other presses such as the *San Francisco Daily Evening Bulletin* printed articles announcing, "PONY EXPRESS, NINE DAYS FROM SAN FRANCISCO TO NEW YORK,"[30] with details of when and where mail would be collected and how much would be charged for letters and telegrams. Truth in advertising was stretched as much in the 1860s as it is in modern times; the promise of nine days in the headline applied to telegraphic dispatches only, but that information was relegated to the small print in the body of the advertisement.

There were those who did not believe that Russell could get his new venture under way in little more than two months. There were others who were convinced that the mail could not travel from Missouri to California in less than two weeks, that bad weather and Indian attacks would quickly put an end to the new experiment.

Russell proved them wrong. The Pony Express took off in a blaze of glory and continued to function successfully despite a vast number of hazards and handicaps. The first ride went down in history as a red-letter event, and papers like the *St. Joseph Free Democrat* expressed the nation's awe and admiration for the new enterprise:

> They (the Pony's footprints) are in California, leaping over its golden sands, treading its busy streets. The courser [swift horse] has unrolled to us the great American panorama, allowed us to glance at the home of one million people. . . . Take out your watch. We are eight days from New York, 18 from London. The race is to the swift.[31]

Ten Days to San Francisco

After weeks of publicity that heralded the Pony Express as "the Greatest Enterprise of Modern Times,"[32] the first run became a much-anticipated event across the country. At the scheduled moment, the afternoon of April 3, large crowds turned out both in San Francisco, California, and St. Joseph, Missouri, to give the Pony Express riders a proper send-off. If all went according to plan, consignments of mail would be carried out of both towns at the same hour, pass somewhere in the middle of the country, and arrive at the opposite terminals two thousand miles away ten days later. Author Howard Driggs, who interviewed several Pony riders later in their lives, observes:

> No wires, no radio, no aeroplane, could keep the nation informed of the progress of the momentous race. It was a pioneer attempt in itself to bring three frontiers— one that lay along the twisting old Missouri; another in the valleys of the Great Salt Lake, and still another in the Eldorado of the Far West—into closer communication. The romance of mystery surrounded the event for days.[33]

East End

In St. Joseph the celebration was especially joyous because the eastern terminus of the route had been kept secret until March 31. Many Americans had assumed that Leavenworth would be chosen, since it was a thriving metropolis, home of Russell, Majors & Waddell, and an important stepping-off point for pioneers heading westward.

But St. Joseph was rapidly developing, too. Built on the banks of the Missouri River, it was another gateway to the West, the western terminus of rails from the East, and the easternmost headquarters of the stage lines. To make it even more attractive as Pony Express headquarters, town officials granted large tracts of land to Russell's company in exchange for the business and attention the Pony Express would generate for the community.

In the days before the run, the presence of several brightly costumed Pony Express riders added to the festive atmosphere in St. Joseph. Dressed in bright red shirts, blue jeans, boots, and spurs, they sauntered through town and attended public dances to the delight of young ladies and the envy of young men who had not qualified for the romantic enterprise. By the afternoon of April 3, most of the young riders had left St. Joseph for their assigned relay stations along the route, but a few remained to give color to the celebration.

As the hour for departure drew near, the first rider led his horse out into the street. Many citizens had taken a holiday from work, and flags and bunting draped the town. No one knows exactly where the run began, although the *St. Joseph Gazette* stated that it began outside the Patee House, an elegant hotel where Russell had his headquarters. Other eyewitnesses maintained it had its start outside the post office, the United States Express office (a freight and parcel company), or the Pony Express livery stable.

Wherever the location, the opening ceremonies took place with much pomp and fanfare. A brass band played and several speeches were made. No one knows if Russell spoke, but Alexander Majors said a few words, and Mayor Merriwether Jeff Thompson got the enterprise under way with a ringing challenge: "The mail must go. Hurled by flesh and blood across 2,000 miles of desolate space—Fort Kearney [sic], Laramie, South Pass, Fort Bridger, Salt Lake City. Neither storms, fatigue, darkness, mountains or Indians, burning sands or snow must stop the precious bags. The mail must go."[34]

Everyone agreed with Thompson, but when the time came for the mail to be loaded onto the pony, an unexpected hitch held up the proceedings. The mail had not yet arrived from the East. En route by train, the messenger carrying it had missed his connection in Detroit.

"A Nervy, Fearless Engineer"

Before the first run of the Pony Express could begin, mail had to be collected from cities in the East and transported to Missouri by train. By a quirk of fate, the special messenger missed his connection the first day, and emergency measures had to be taken to get him to St. Joseph. Author Roy S. Bloss describes the final breathtaking leg of the rail trip between Hannibal and St. Joseph in *Pony Express—The Great Gamble*.

"[Roadmaster George H.] Davis ordered all trains off the main line and every switch spiked. He selected Ad Clark, a 'nervy, fearless engineer,' to make the run at the throttle. His train consisted of the woodburner engine *Missouri*, with tender and one car.

Fuel agents between Hannibal and St. Joseph were instructed to stand by for loading the tender 'in less than no time.' Engineer Clark received instructions equally terse: make a speed record that would last 50 years!

When the messenger arrived at Hannibal from Detroit and climbed aboard with several passengers, the little train took off in a cloud of steam and smoke. The first 70 miles was over fairly straight and level roadbed, and here Ad Clark's speed was estimated at a frightening 60 miles per hour. Then came Macon, and C. S. Coleman's fuel stop. On the platform men were waiting with armloads of wood. In just 15 seconds the tender was replenished and the train jerked down the track, rapidly gaining speed. The passengers gripped their seats as the car crazily rocked sideways, threatening to dump them on the floor.

Ahead was the steep grade down to the Chariton River. Ad Clark took it 'like an avalanche,' a hot blast of fire shooting out the stack and wood sparks streaming backwards like crimson snowflakes. . . .

A few minutes past 7:00 P.M., the little train pulled into the St. Joseph depot. Clark 'stepped majestically from his iron horse,' looking mussed up, grimy and grand. Unbelievably, he had made the long run in only four hours and 51 minutes. For the instant, he was the hero, the Pony Express almost forgotten."

An hour passed. The crowd grew restless. The band played a repertoire of lively songs, and the rider showed off his horse, a "bright bay mare"[35] said to be named Sylph. It wore a specially made saddle and a leather mail carrier called a *mochila*. Soon, however, so many souvenir hunters had plucked hair from the pony's mane and tail that it had to be returned to its stall. A writer for the *St. Joseph Weekly West*, who did not look closely enough to realize that the animal was a female, reported, "The little pony was almost robbed of his tail."[36]

Finally, a few minutes past seven o'clock, the shriek of a whistle signaled the train's arrival. The horse was once again led to the street, the messenger from the East hurriedly surrendered his pouch to town officials, and the contents were locked into the *mochila*. They included forty-nine letters, five telegrams, and copies of Eastern newspapers printed on tissue paper to reduce their bulk and weight. Together, all weighed less than fifteen pounds.

With the cheers of the crowd ringing in his ears, the rider mounted, shook hands with William Russell, and spurred his horse to a gallop down Jules Street. The first ride was under way. Now only time would tell if the great experiment would be successful or not.

The First Rider

The occasion was momentous, the day unforgettable, but the identity of the rider who swung himself into the saddle and galloped away down Jules Street remains in dispute even today. Seven different men—Alexander Carlyle, Charles Cliff, Gus Cliff, John Frye, Jack Keetley, Johnson William Richardson, and Henry Wallace—were named at one time or other as riding the first leg of the journey out of St. Joseph. Over time, however, possibilities were narrowed down to two, Richardson and Frye.

Company records were lost over the years, but the *Weekly West* of April 7 clearly states that Richardson was the man, describing him as "formerly a sailor, and a man accustomed to every description of hardship, having sailed for years among the snows of the Northern ocean."[37] A thorough study of period letters, diaries, scrapbooks, and newspapers, initiated by organizers of the St. Joseph Pony Express Celebration in 1923, backed that conclusion, and most historical sources agreed that the rider was Richardson.

Eyewitnesses, however, including several Pony Express riders, claimed that John Frye manned the first leg of the race that day. "I ought to know, I was right there," stated Charles Cliff when interviewed years later. "John used to ride in all the races in these parts. . . . Richardson was a kind of a sailor. Does it stand to reason that they would have him ride when they could get a race-horse rider to start the biggest race that was ever run in this country?"[38]

To buttress Cliff's assertions, Richardson himself later denied that he was the first rider. He claimed that his brother, who owned the livery stable, had put him on the horse for the trip to the ferry just out of town. At the river, Frye took over for the ride west. Absolute certainty can never be achieved at this point, but Frye seems the most likely holder of the honor.

The Mail Heads West

Whether Frye or Richardson, the dash out of St. Joseph slowed to a halt on the east bank of the "Big Muddy," the Missouri River, where the rider had to board a waiting ferry to get to the far shore. On board he changed clothes in

The identity of the first Pony Express rider to leave St. Joseph, Missouri, is still disputed by historians.

preparation for the hard ride ahead. Pony rider Jack Keetley later wrote:

> We always rode out of town with silver mounted trappings decorating both man and horse and regular uniforms with plated horn, pistol, scabbard, and belt, etc., and gay flower-worked leggings and plated jingling spurs resembling, for all the world, a fantastic circus rider. This was all changed, however, as soon as we got on to the boat. We had a room in which to change and to leave the trappings in until our return.[39]

Night was falling by the time the rider left the ferry. Due to the late arrival of the mail, he was two and a half hours behind schedule and had to ride hard to try and make up that time. His route followed the well-traveled Oregon–California Trail and led him into northern Kansas Territory, where he exchanged one exhausted horse for another every ten to fifteen miles at stations set up for that purpose. Sometimes these outposts were isolated and primitive. Sometimes they were located in a small town or community.

The station at the settlement of Seneca was his final stop. Here he turned the mail over to sixteen-year-old Don Rising, who had been impatiently awaiting the arrival for over an hour. The first rider had made up three-quarters of an hour of lost time, but Rising was still behind schedule. He galloped off down the road and traveled the rest of the

Some Pony Express riders traveled along the well-established Oregon–California Trail.

night, arriving in Marysville, Kansas—a town that according to one traveler thrived "by selling whiskey to ruffians of all descriptions"[40]—about 8:15 A.M. on April 4. There he handed the mail pouch to Jack Keetley, who had to ford at least one river and travel a stretch of road crowded with wagon trains before arriving at his final destination, Big Sandy Station in Nebraska Territory. (Some sources state that Keetley rode only to Hollenberg's Station, the last Pony Express stop in Kansas.)

West End

On the same day and at almost the same hour that the residents of St. Joseph were preparing their send-off for the westbound rider, the people of San Francisco prepared to speed the eastbound mail on its way. At 4 P.M., a "clean-limbed hardy little nankeen-colored [yellow or buff] pony,"[41] decorated with miniature flags and carrying saddlebags lettered with OVER-LAND PONY EXPRESS, was led out in front of the Alta Telegraph Company on Montgomery Street. The rider, James Randall, was so nervous that he mounted from the wrong side, but the crowd cheered nevertheless, and horse and rider trotted off down the street.

Randall was not a Pony Express man and the horse was not a Pony Express racer, but they had to travel only a short distance through town to the steamboat *Antelope*. "He (the pony) will make short work, and probably be back tonight, but by proxy he will put the west behind his heels."[42] claimed the *Daily Alta California* newspaper. The steamer carried the mail up the Sacramento River to the town of Sacramento, official western terminus of the Pony Express.

Sacramento had developed into a commercial and transportation center during the California gold rush and had been designated the state's capital in 1854. The mushrooming town was the natural choice for Russell's Pony Express western terminal. According to Chapman:

> No city in the state partook more of the varied characteristics that made California unique. The steamers that came up from the Bay brought along some of San Francisco's touch of cosmopolitanism. The miners who flocked in from the "green hills" for supplies and entertainment added their touch of the frontier. . . . Part mining camp, though miles removed from the golden gravel; a port many miles from the sea; the financial hub of a wheel set with gold; a trading center where men bartered with legal tender unminted, Sacramento teemed with life.[43]

The *Antelope* docked in Sacramento at 2 A.M. on April 4 in the middle of a rainstorm. Here, in contrast to St. Joseph and San Francisco, no one was present to see the first official Pony Express rider, William Hamilton, pick up the *mochila* with its eighty-five letters and headed off up the dark, muddy road.

The Great Relay Race

William Hamilton and Warren Upson possessed the dedication and determination that characterized all riders as they helped launch the first run of the Pony Express. As Howard R. Driggs describes in *The Pony Express Goes Through*, both men did their best to meet every challenge, knowing that the nation was waiting to see if "the Pony" could maintain the breakneck schedule it had set for itself.

"Old Fort Sutter [outside Sacramento] was soon passed, and on up the American River [William Hamilton] made his way, the brave little horse splashing along the rain-soaked road. At Folsom a fresh mount was ready, and on the young rider went over the hills, clipping down the miles that lay between him and another young American whose pony's hoofs were beating a tattoo on the same trail westward. The great relay race was on.

Placerville—called 'Hangtown' in Vigilante Days—was wide-awake when Billy Hamilton came crashing up to the station there. Cheered to the echo, he leaped on to another spirited horse, and was away on the road for old Sportsmans' Hall, the first Home station, about sixty miles west of Sacramento. And the intrepid young Californian made the end of his run, despite the dark and the rain, almost on schedule.

Warren Upson . . . was waiting there to carry the mail on over the Sierras. It was the toughest part of the whole trail. A heavy spring snow that had fallen had blocked even the stages on that part of the route. Could the pony rider make it? . . . Half-a-dozen sturdy ponies, selected for endurance rather than speed, were scattered along the mountain trail to help him win. It took all the energy they had and all the vigor of Warren's stout body to battle through. . . . Hours were consumed in the battling work, but finally the crest was reached. Lake Tahoe smiled from the high mountain valley on the Nevada side of the granite peaks of the high Sierras. The worst of the ride was over; the bets against the plucky pony rider were lost."

Nevertheless, he was the first rider in the eastbound direction, and the western leg of the Pony Express was officially under way. (Some early accounts state that the first rider was Harry Roff, but the weight of evidence favors Hamilton.)

Cautiously, but making the best speed possible, Hamilton trotted out of Sacramento toward the foothills, stopping to pick up a fresh horse at Five Mile House, Fifteen Mile House, and then at Mormon Tavern. By 6:45 A.M. he was in Placerville, half an hour ahead of schedule. An hour later he had reached his final station, Sportsman's Hall, a popular inn and stage stop in the Sierra Nevada foothills.

At Sportsman's Hall, the second rider, Warren Upson, took over. Upson was the son of the editor of the *Sacramento Daily Union* newspaper, an experienced horseman, and well acquainted with mountain travel in all seasons. He needed all his expertise, however, setting out in a snowstorm that became a blizzard as he climbed to higher altitudes. An icy wind lashed his face; the snow blinded him. The mountain pass was closed to all other traffic, but he forged ahead, breaking a trail through enormous drifts, leading his pony when necessary. Authors Raymond and Mary Lund Settle observe: "During the eighteen months the Pony Express was in operation, there were longer and more dangerous rides . . . but none ever surpassed this one. For sheer courage and determination in the face of natural hazards Upson's first ride stands in a class by itself."[44]

Late on the night of April 5, an exhausted Upson rode into Carson City, eighty-five miles from where he began. There he passed the *mochila* on to his successor, Robert "Pony Bob" Haslam. Twenty-year-old Haslam, who soon gained a reputation for being one of the most daring and resourceful riders, whipped up his horse and dashed off. His relay, distin-guished by scorching heat, dead-end canyons, and hostile Indians, would become known as some of the harshest and most dangerous territory of the whole route.

Over Hills and Plains

Mile by mile, hour by hour, the riders sped along a course that had been mapped out by Russell and Majors earlier in the year. It was one of the longest overland routes in the world, 1,966 miles from St. Joseph to Sacramento, second only to Butterfield's Overland Mail route to the south. Essentially, the Pony Express path followed the Oregon–California Trail from Missouri, cutting through parts of present-day Kansas and spanning what would become the states of Nebraska and Wyoming, with a dip into the northern corner of Colorado.

Animals were plentiful in this region and included prairie dogs, coyotes, and prong-horn antelope. "A word now on the antelope. I liked him when I first saw him . . . and since I dined with him (that is, off of him), my esteem has ripened into affection,"[45] noted Horace Greeley when he traveled through the region in 1859. Doubtless, Pony Express riders enjoyed pronghorn meat as well, when they paused at a home station to eat a meal.

West of Fort Kearny, Nebraska, riders followed the Platte River for two hundred miles. From this point westward, most stretches of trail were lonely and unsettled, although riders passed the settlements of Scottsbluff, Nebraska; Salt Lake City, Utah; and Carson City, Nevada. Sometimes the route ran through wooded areas. Sometimes it ran through rolling hills and open plains, where riders saw land such as that described by British explorer Sir Richard Burton as he traveled across the United States by stage in 1860:

The soil is rich, clayey, and dotted with swamps and "slews" [sloughs]. . . . The dryer portions were a Gulistan [rose garden] of bright red, blue, and white flowers, the purple aster, and the mallow . . . Buffalo herds were behind the hills, but we were too full of sleep to follow them.

The plain was dotted with blanched skulls and bones, which would have made a splendid bonfire.[46]

In western Wyoming, riders encountered the Rocky Mountains and crossed the Continental Divide, the invisible dividing

Crossing the Rocky Mountains was a hazardous experience for Pony Express riders and other travelers.

line that separates streams flowing west toward the Pacific Ocean from streams flowing eastward. Heading southwest, they entered Utah Territory and pounded across scorched and barren desert, where, as Burton colorfully writes, "The hair of this unlovely skin was sage and greasewood: it was warted with sand-heaps; in places mottled with bald and horrid patches of salt soil, while in others minute crystals of salt, glistening like diamond-dust in the sunlight, covered tracts of moist and oozy mud."[47] Beyond Utah lay arid Nevada, then the rugged Sierra Nevadas, and finally Sacramento, the other end of the trail.

Unrecorded Passage

Each section of the country had its unique characteristics, and riders undoubtedly had many opportunities to enjoy brilliant sunsets, breathtaking mountaintop vistas, and the wild beauty of frozen lakes and snowy fields as they traveled east and west. Undoubtedly, many took what they saw for granted, particularly on the first ride when they were focused on getting to the next station as quickly as possible.

Perhaps for that reason, no one bothered to identify and remember the rock, meadow, or grove of trees where east- and westbound Pony Express riders met and passed each other on the evening of April 8, 1860. No one knows whether the two men acknowledged each other's presence, perhaps with a wave and a shout of excitement. Some greeting seems likely, since both were aware of the momentous nature of their journey, and neither had had time to become indifferent to the pulse-pounding race that became almost routine in the coming months. Whatever their reactions were, experts estimate that

their meeting took place somewhere on the eastern slope of the Rocky Mountains in Wyoming. The exact time and place will always be lost to history.

The names of the two riders who met that night have been lost to history as well. They, and many of the men who carried the mail across the central part of the route even on that first famous trip, are not known or celebrated. Most were included in company records, but records were lost. References to some have been found, but little or nothing is known about the men linked to the names.

The Relay System

William Russell set up the Pony Express so that no man or horse rode the entire length of the country. Each rider shuttled back and forth on a specific seventy-five-mile stretch of trail, changing horses every ten to fifteen miles, stopping at a home station at each end to rest and wait until it was time to carry the mail in the opposite direction. Some men were assigned one specific segment of the trail and seldom went beyond it except in rare cases of emergency. For instance, Pony Bob Haslam commonly rode back and forth between Friday's Station near the foot of Lake Tahoe and Buckland's Station, seventy-five miles to the east. (After Fort Churchill was established a few miles west of Buckland's in the summer of 1860, it became Haslam's home station at that end of the run.)

Other riders changed territory occasionally. Don Rising rode between Granada and Marysville, Kansas, then later transferred to the run between Big Sandy and Fort Kearny. William Frederick Fisher first rode between Ruby Valley and Schell Creek in Nevada but was later transferred to work between Salt Lake City and Rush Valley, Utah.

Pony Express riders changed horses every ten to fifteen miles.

For the most part, however, each run was short and well defined. Although unexpected events could take riders by surprise—being caught in a storm or running into Indians, for example—after a time most must have known their section of trail so well that they could navigate its length with little thought or concentration.

The relay system was simple, but the length of the trail, and the fact that mail was sent out from both ends of the route weekly (and later twice weekly), meant that riders and *mochilas* were constantly shuttling back and forth at different points along the trail. For example, before the first runs were completed on April 13 and 14, second runs began from both St. Joseph and Sacramento in accordance with Russell's weekly schedule. Thus, two riders would have been heading east at the same time—perhaps in Nevada and Nebraska—while two men galloped west. When runs were changed to a twice weekly schedule, a series of Pony Express riders were always crisscrossing the country, meeting each other at various points depending on the day and conditions under which they traveled.

"Long Live the Pony!"

At 4:30 P.M. on April 13, John Frye galloped back toward St. Joseph, boarded the Missouri River ferry, and completed the last leg of the eastbound mail relay. The *mochila* he carried

"Keeping to the Schedule"

No one knew exactly what would happen on the first run of the Pony Express, but riders were expected to keep to a strict schedule despite unexpected complications or obstacles. Raymond and Mary Lund Settle include the assigned agenda in *Saddles and Spurs: The Pony Express Saga*.

"A schedule, as exacting as that of a railroad timetable, was set up, and each rider was under rigid orders to keep it, day and night, fair weather and foul. Allowance was made for nothing, not even attack by Indians. Their motto was 'The mail must go through,' and it did except in a very few, rare cases. As published in the St. Joseph *Weekly West* the schedule for the first run was as follows:

Marysville	12 hours
Fort Kearny	34 hours
Fort Laramie	80 hours
Fort Bridger	108 hours
Great Salt Lake	124 hours
Camp Floyd	128 hours
Carson City	188 hours
Placerville	226 hours
Sacramento	234 hours
San Francisco	240 hours"

had changed horses about 190 times since it left San Francisco ten days before. As Frye entered town, crowds roared their welcome and appreciation, cheering the first round-trip mail delivery by Pony Express to be completed. Frye deposited the letters from San Francisco, and a grand celebration began. One author describes: "He was greeted with loud cheers and the clanging of church bells. At the Patee House . . . the cannon again boomed a thunderous salute, while local militiamen, dressed in uniform, paraded the streets and fired their rifles. Bonfires and fireworks added to the combustive celebration."[48]

One day earlier—April 12 at 3:30 P.M.—and two thousand miles across the country, Warren Upson again slapped a *mochila* of mail across his horse, leaped into the saddle, and spurred off across the Sierras. This time he was heading westward, however, and the mail he carried was the first batch that had originated in St. Joseph nine days before. Snow was no longer falling in the mountains, but the trail was still treacherous, and he had to flounder through unbroken drifts to detour

around a wagon train that was passing along the trail. Twenty-two hours of hard riding later, he reached Sportsman's Hall and handed the pouch over to William Hamilton for the run to Sacramento. Hamilton hurried off down the road. News of his impending arrival had been telegraphed from Carson City, so a cheering crowd awaited him both in Placerville and in the state capital.

Approaching Sacramento, William Hamilton's arrival was as festive and celebratory as John Frye's had been in St. Joseph. No one had remembered to put together a welcoming party until the last minute, but a scramble of activity produced flags and banners, signs in windows, and a committee of eighty citizens and fifteen militiamen ready to form a double line along the road over which Hamilton would pass. Crowds gathered on street corners, boys and men climbed lampposts and roofs, and women hung over balconies in eager anticipation of the rider's appearance.

Shortly after five o'clock in the evening, a cloud of dust was detected on the Fort Sutter

Road outside of town. A mounted welcoming committee raced out to meet Hamilton, engulfed him in their enthusiasm, then escorted him into the city center. One author notes, "Being mounted upon fresh horses they quickly put Hamilton and his weary pony to the rear. Much to the disgust of both of them they had to 'eat dust' the remainder of the way in."[49]

When Hamilton and his escort reached Sutter's Fort, cannons boomed, church bells rang, and the crowd cheered. The rider proceeded to the Express office, where the Sacramento mail was taken out and distributed. Then, carrying the *mochila*, Hamilton and his horse hurried to the dock where the *Antelope* waited to depart. Making a record run, it arrived in San Francisco shortly after midnight on April 14.

Despite the lateness of the hour, another celebration awaited Hamilton. Bonfires and fireworks popped and crackled in street intersections, and a large crowd gathered at the dock. Hamilton rode his pony down the gangplank amid a tumult of cheers, bells, and rockets, then was caught up in a noisy parade made up of an eighteen-piece band, several fire companies, and a group of citizens on foot and horseback. The band struck up "See the Conquering Hero Comes," and everyone moved off to the Alta Telegraph Company, the final destination of the mail. The *San Francisco Daily Evening Bulletin* gave a colorful and detailed account of the evening:

> The crowd cheered till their throats were sore; the Band played as if they would crack their cheeks. . . . While the twenty-five letters that were brought were being distributed, the speechmakers were proceeding to uncork the bottles of their eloquence. . . . [But the pony] looked a bit sleepy, thought of his

oats, and uttered a loud *neigh*. So the speeches were corked down again, the speech-makers tied comforters around their throats . . . the rag-tag-and-bob-tail [crowd] took something warm, the morning papers went to press, the crowd to bed and the Pony to his stable. . . . Long live the Pony![50]

The efficient Pony Express service advertised in this newspaper was a popular topic of conversation in towns along the route.

PONY EXPRESS!

CHANGE OF TIME!   REDUCED RATES!

10 Days to San Francisco!

LETTERS

WILL BE RECEIVED AT THE

OFFICE, 84 BROADWAY,

NEW YORK,

Up to **4** P. M. every TUESDAY,

AND

Up to **2½** P. M. every SATURDAY,

Which will be forwarded to connect with the PONY EXPRESS leaving ST. JOSEPH, Missouri,

Every WEDNESDAY and SATURDAY at 11 P. M.

TELEGRAMS

Sent to Fort Kearney on the mornings of MONDAY and FRIDAY, will connect with **PONY** leaving St. Joseph, WEDNESDAYS and SATURDAYS.

EXPRESS CHARGES.

LETTERS weighing half ounce or under.............$1 00
For every additional half ounce or fraction of an ounce 1 00
In all cases to be enclosed in 10 cent Government Stamped Envelopes,
And all **Express CHARGES** Pre-paid.

☞ PONY EXPRESS ENVELOPES For Sale at our Office.

WELLS, FARGO & CO., Ag'ts.

New York, Ju'y 1, 1861.

The World Talks "Pony"

The first run of the Pony Express had taken place in ten days, exactly as William Russell had hoped when he planned his experiment two months before. The venture had all the earmarks of a rousing success and was doubly impressive because relays of riders were again on the trail, carrying the second week's mail delivery across country.

For days the public could talk of little else. The *Daily Evening Bulletin* proclaimed, "The 'Pony' was all the toast. . . . At every man's dinner table, men, women, and children talked *pony*."[51] In Washington Congress buzzed with the news that the central route had proven suitable as an alternative to Butterfield's southerly course. Newspapers took note of the new venture; editorials applauded the foresight of the men who had closed the gap between East and West. As time passed, European publications printed descriptions of "Le Poney Post" and dime-store novels delighted readers with tales of the stouthearted saddlemen.

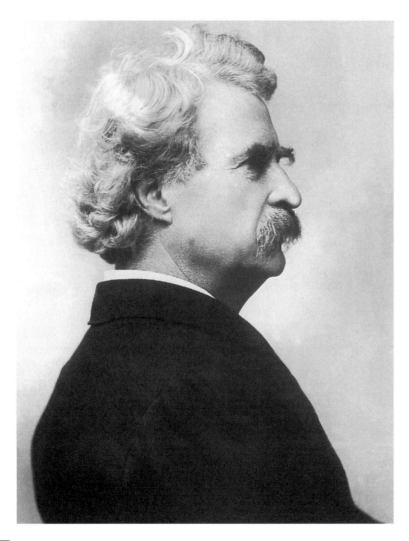

Author Mark Twain glorified the Pony Express rider in his book Roughing It.

Even renowned authors mentioned the Express in their writings. The most famous was Mark Twain, who provided a word picture of the great adventure in *Roughing It*, written after he saw a Pony Express rider on a trip out west.

All interest was taken up in stretching our necks and watching for the "pony-rider"— the fleet messenger who sped across the continent from St. Joe to Sacramento, carrying letters nineteen hundred miles in eight days! Think of that for perishable horse and human flesh and blood to do! . . . No matter what time of the day or night his watch came on, and no matter whether it was winter or summer, raining, snowing, hailing, or sleeting, or whether his "beat" was a level straight road or a crazy trail over mountain crags and precipices, or whether it led through peaceful regions or regions that swarmed with hostile Indians, he must be always ready to leap into the saddle and be off like the wind! There was no idling time for a pony-rider on duty.[52]

The men of the Pony Express were American heroes, respected, admired, and beloved. The success of the enterprise lay on their shoulders, and most proved capable of bearing that responsibility in the days and months ahead.

Fearless in the Saddle

The organizers of the Pony Express realized that carrying the mail at top speed across wide, untamed stretches of the continent would not be easy, and they wanted the best men they could find for the job. Between February and April 1860, hundreds of young men applied for the position. No more than eighty were hired, and these were tough, capable individuals who were drawn by a love of adventure rather than the promise of fame or high pay. One former bullwhacker (oxen driver), William Campbell, remembered his motivation to join:

> Driving slow oxen seemed pretty tame compared with jumping on spirited ponies and going full tilt along the old trail, past the emigrant trains and freight outfits, or even bands of Indians. I was just eighteen, and boylike, craved such excitement; so I mustered up courage to ask Mr. Majors to let me "ride the Pony Express."[53]

To Be a Rider

Many details of the Pony Express riders have been lost over time. For instance, if a woman or an African American rode for the company, no record of their service remains. There was much public interest in the great experiment, but epic developments relating to civil war overshadowed all other events in 1860–61. Newspapers of the day tended to focus on war news, lengthy political speeches, and editorials. After the war, the Pony Express was all but forgotten for half a century, while particulars of the riders' identities and day-to-day lives faded from memory.

A significant amount of information remains, however. Twenty years was the stated minimum age for a Pony rider, and in the beginning that qualification was closely observed by at least some division superintendents. One plainsman recalls, "I asked my brother to go with me to the station to see if I could get a job as a rider. I had ridden a [local] mail route for a year—from 1859 to 1860. The agent, or manager, at Kearney [sic] said they would not hire any rider under 20 years of age."[54] Soon, however, age ceased to be an issue. Many riders were younger than twenty; most were about nineteen years of age. David Robert Jay was the youngest, hired at the age of thirteen. A few, such as William Boulton, were as old as thirty-five or forty when they were hired.

Maturity was more important than age. Riders were expected to be highly responsible, fearless, and hardworking. Being single was a plus, since riders would be on the road much of the time with no time to devote to a family. High moral standards were required. Alexander Majors was an upright, religious man, and he expected the same from his employees. Riders were given a Bible upon joining the Pony Express and were required to take the well-known Majors's pledge:

I . . . do hereby swear, before the Great and Living God, that during my engagement, and while I am an employee of Russell, Majors & Waddell, I will, under no circumstances, use profane language; that I will drink no intoxicating liquors; that I will not quarrel or fight with any other employee of the firm, and that in every respect I will conduct myself honestly, be faithful to my duties, and so direct all my acts as to win the confidence of my employers. So help me God.[55]

Despite Majors's efforts, many riders undoubtedly broke this pledge as soon as they took to the trail. Traveler Richard Burton testified from firsthand experience: "His [Majors's] meritorious efforts to reform the morals of the land have not yet put forth even the bud of promise. . . . I scarcely ever saw a sober [stage] driver; as for profanity—the Western equivalent for hard swearing—they would make the blush of shame crimson the cheek of the old Isis bargee [London bargeman]. . . . "[56] Still, many riders took their promise seriously and lived more upright lives than did ordinary cowboys or prospectors.

Physical attributes were as important as moral ones. Riders needed to be healthy, slight in build (no more than 125 pounds), and wiry, with unusual strength and stamina. Even in this area, standards relaxed somewhat over time, as rider Campbell, hired sometime after the commencement of the service, attested: "I was over the average height, and I weighed one hundred and forty pounds. In fact, with my six feet, I was one of the tallest men in the service, but they weren't so particular that winter, if they could find men who could get the mail through."[57]

A Pennsylvania infantry stands in formation in 1861. Civil War events overshadowed the novelty and success of the Pony Express.

Pony Express riders had to be rigorous outdoorsmen as well as excellent horsemen. At least some division superintendents conducted tryouts for applicants. In Sacramento and Salt Lake City, local youths took to the streets to show off their riding skills in front of a critical supervisor and crowds of curious bystanders.

Garb and Gear

Even the most qualified riders could not make good time if they were encumbered by heavy clothes and tack (equipment for a horse including saddle and bridle). The first riders out of St. Joseph were asked to wear a type of uniform that included high-topped boots, broad-brimmed hats, even white buckskin gloves, but comfort and practicality were more of a priority than fashion on the trail. Men usually changed into ordinary work clothes as soon as they were out of the public eye.

Most wore cloth trousers tucked into boots, a work shirt made of buckskin (soft grayish yellow leather made from deerskin), and a hat. Mark Twain describes them as "flying light." "The rider's dress was thin and fitted close; he wore a 'roundabout' [short, closing-fitting jacket] and a skull cap, and tucked his pantaloons into his boot-tops like a race rider."[58] In the winter some men wore a buckskin jacket, others a complete buckskin suit with hair on the outside to help repel rain. Lightweight clothing was always important, as extra weight quickly tired the hard-working horses.

For the sake of the horses, loads did not exceed 165 pounds, including rider, gear, saddle, and mail. In the beginning, each rider was given two revolvers, a bowie knife, and lightweight rifle for protection, plus a small horn to be blown as he neared an upcoming

A monument to Pony Express riders and horses is displayed at the Old Sacramento State Historic Park in California.

relay station. That signal would alert the station keeper to have a rested horse saddled and out in the yard.

All this equipment proved weighty and unwieldy, however. Riders soon relied on their horse's pounding hoofs and a "coyote yell" to announce their arrival, and on their animal's speed to escape dangers along the trail. Most riders carried little with them but a loaded Colt revolver and an extra bullet-loaded cylinder for emergencies.

Saddle and *Mochila*

Since an ordinary western saddle was a heavy piece of equipment, Pony Express managers substituted a specially designed model with an abbreviated skirt and stirrups, a broad, short horn, and a low cantle (the raised rear part of the seat), designed along the lines of a jockey saddle. It weighed much less than an ordinary saddle but was strong and roomy enough to be moderately comfortable during a long, pounding ride. The designer of the saddle remains unknown, but the articles themselves were constructed by several reputable suppliers including well-known entrepreneur Israel Landis, who provided saddles to many westward-bound pioneers from his famous saddlery in St. Joseph.

Over the saddle, riders tossed another specially designed article—the leather *mochila* (sometimes spelled *machila*), or saddlebag, that held the mail. Regular mail pouches were seldom if ever used by Pony Express riders because of their awkward size and shape and because they caused delay in changing horses.

The *mochila* was a rectangle of leather about one-eighth inch thick with slits for the saddle's cantle and horn to project through. It was not attached anywhere and could be taken off by simply lifting upward. On each side, two slim locked boxes—*cantinas*—hung fore and aft of the rider's thighs. Station keepers at either end of the line held keys to three of the *cantinas*, and cross-country mail was locked inside. Mail that was picked up and delivered at various points along the trail was placed in the fourth. Together, saddle and empty *mochila* weighed about thirteen pounds.

Pony Express rider Jack Keetley later described the *mochila* as he remembered it:

> We rode into the office and put on the mail, which consisted of four small leather sacks six by twelve inches, fastened on to a

The Saddlemaker

No record exists that identifies the designer of the Pony Express saddle and *mochila*, but a large number were constructed by Israel Landis, a noted St. Joseph saddle maker. Arthur Chapman gives a few details of Landis's life and personality in *The Pony Express*.

"Israel Landis, who turned out the Pony Express saddles, was a well-known character, not alone in St. Joe, but along the trail. He started business 'at the sign of the Big Saddle,' in 1844. When the rush of '49ers began, he rented three buildings, to keep up with the expansion of his business, and hired some of the emigrants who were compelled to winter in St. Joe. In front of his shop was a large wooden frame in which he inserted each week a 'poem' advertising his wares. These bits of doggerel became famous all the way to California and were sung or chanted along the trail. Everyone stopped to see what there was new in 'Big Saddle Poetry' in St. Joe. The verses usually started off something like this:

> If a good saddle you would find,
>
> One that's just suited to your mind,
>
> You need not to St. Louis go,
>
> For you can get one in St. Joe."

square macheir [variation on the word *mochila*] which was put over the saddle. The sacks were locked with little brass locks . . . and the sacks were sewed to the macheir, one in front and one behind each leg of the rider.[59]

The *mochila* was treated like the baton in a relay race. When a rider came into a relay station, he would jump off his horse, slip the *mochila* off the saddle, toss it over the saddle of a fresh mount, and with one swift leap be on his way. Horses that were well rested were often already on the move, and the rider had to jump on while the animal was breaking into a gallop. Mark Twain describes the process in *Roughing It*: "As he came crashing up to the station where stood two men holding fast a fresh, impatient steed, the transfer of rider and mail-bag was made in a twinkling of an eye, and away flew the eager pair and were out of sight before the spectator could get hardly the ghost of a look."[60]

Rider Gus Cliff gave at least one of the reasons the riders sped out of the stations in a cloud of dust—many horses were so highly spirited as to be almost wild. "It was common to find that you had drawn a bucking horse when you started out of the station," he says. "That was one reason why we gave them the spurs right from the start and kept them going."[61]

The Mail

Mail that was carried by Pony Express was kept as light as possible. Dispatches, letters, and even newspapers were printed on special tissue paper, then wrapped in oiled silk (silk made waterproof by saturation with boiled oil) to keep them dry in wet weather or while the rider was fording a river. The maximum weight for any shipment of mail was twenty pounds. As previously planned, letter writers paid $5 per half ounce for Pony Express delivery at first, although charges were reduced to $2 per half ounce in April 1861.

Two-thirds of the mail carried by the Pony Express consisted of business letters and newspapers. Californians were more prone to use the service than were easterners, perhaps because it reduced their sense of isolation. "California letter writers have more than half covered the cost of several trips, and if as many letters were sent from this end of the line westward, the express would now pay,"[62] writes one observer in St. Louis, Missouri, remarking on the chronically shaky financial status of the enterprise.

Some of the mail was telegrams, which had been transmitted from the East by wire to St. Joseph or Fort Kearny, Nebraska, the outermost reaches of telegraph lines in the East. These messages had to be physically carried to Carson City, where telegraph service resumed.

Some of the mail was government dispatches, since European diplomats stationed in Asia could communicate faster with their homelands via the Pony Express than by sending messages by ship around Cape Horn or across Panama. Reportedly, the British government, at war with China in 1860, paid up to $135 postage on some important documents sent by Pony Express, since it was their safest and most speedy route for transmitting news between the Far East and London.

As time passed, the Pony Express became more popular. Between November 1860 and April 1861, an average of forty-one letters per ride were carried to San Francisco from the eastern United States; by October 1861 that number had climbed to ninety. William Campbell remembered: "Sometimes we carried as high as two hundred and fifty letters,"[63] but even those numbers may be conservative.

Riders carried telegrams between regions of the country that were not connected by telegraph communication.

The chief postal clerk in Atchison, Kansas (eastern terminus of the route during the last months of the Pony Express), testified that during the final six or seven weeks of the enterprise, about 350 letters per trip were carried from the Pacific coast.

Over the course of their runs, Pony Express riders successfully delivered almost thirty-five thousand pieces of mail. Yet through no fault of theirs, the service failed completely in one important sense—it lost money from the beginning. First, the undertaking was handicapped by not having sufficient offices where mail could be collected. Citizens in California who would have liked to use the Pony Express had no way of getting their letters to Sacramento or San Francisco,

the two main offices in that state. Second, William Russell failed to calculate the high cost of operating his enterprise—$25,000 to $30,000 a month—and thus did not set his charges high enough. At $5 a half ounce, over a hundred thousand pieces of mail would have had to be carried across the country in the eighteen months the Pony Express operated in order to meet expenses. Instead, the company lost at least $200,000; about $13 per letter during the course of the Pony's run.

The Horses

Despite the title of their operation—the Pony Express—Russell, Majors, and Waddell never intended for their riders to use ponies, which are by definition smaller and lighter than ordinary horses. Understanding that the safety of their men as well as the success of the venture hinged on the speed and stamina of their animals, they spared no expense to get the best full-sized horses possible.

All of the animals were sturdy and tough with plenty of spirit. William Campbell later stated: "The men who bought the horses knew their business. Sometimes we used to say that the company had bought up every mean, bucking, kicking horse that could be found, but they were good stock and could outrun anything along the trail."[64]

Most animals were required to run only ten miles at a stretch, but such a gallop was a grueling experience even for a thoroughbred. Journalist and author William Lightfoot Visscher, a Civil War veteran, writes, "He [the rider's horse] came dashing into the station flecked with foam, nostrils dilated, and every hair reeking with perspiration, while his flanks thumped at every breath."[65] Naturally, animals were given plenty of food, water, and rest before they were once again required to run another leg of the relay.

Since horses might become tired, ill, or injured, five hundred mounts were purchased at the start, and others were added over time. East of Fort Laramie, most Pony Express horses were bred in Kentucky and purchased from the cavalry. In the West, mustangs were chosen, since they were descendants of fleet-footed Arabian horses brought to the New World by the Spanish.

To get good animals, Russell paid top price, $150 to $200 a head—about $87,000 in total. At the time, a man might have paid $50 for an ordinary mount. No expense was spared for feed, either. Horses were given grain and hay, in contrast with Indian ponies who lived on range grass. One Pony Express rider believed he experienced the benefit of

Four-Footed Heroes

No expense was spared to obtain the best horses for the Pony Express, and the strength and endurance that went into their breeding shone through in their performance on the trail. Some animals proved to be as courageous and dedicated as their riders, as Elijah Wilson explains in Howard R. Driggs's *The Pony Express Goes Through*.

"The horses that carried both mail and riders in that famous relay race, by the way, are entitled to unstinted praise. If it hadn't been for them, there wouldn't have been any Pony Express; and if all the stories of those four-footed heroes could be told, there would be a thrilling series of them.

There was Black Billy, for instance, who always made a home run. He never failed to bring his rider through. One day he came in carrying two arrows, one in his shoulder, another in his flank; but he reached the station with his rider. . . .

And there was another horse, a gray one—'American Boy' I believe they called him—a high-spirited steed. One day when they were changing mail, he broke away and went dashing along the trail, leaving the hostlers and rider at the station. But he did not fail in his duty, even though he was riderless. He carried the mail clear through to the next station, beating the pony rider, who had hurried after him on another horse."

his horse's diet while being chased by hostile Indians during one of his runs. "[My horse's] grain-fed muscles got me out of the danger of their arrows and the few old guns they had. Their grass-fed ponies couldn't keep long within gunshot."[66]

Conditions of the Ride

Since most riders were hired by division superintendents in a particular region, they commonly rode a section of trail in country with which they were familiar. For instance, those individuals who rode the midwestern parts of the relay were often from the Midwest. Those who rode in the West were often from the West, raised on ranches and accustomed to the demands of the frontier. In Utah, many were Mormons whose families had carved homes for themselves out of the desert. There were exceptions to the rule, however. Michael Whalen, who rode in the vicinity of Salt Lake City, was born in New York City. Thomas J. "Happy Tom" Ranahan, who rode in Wyoming, was born in Ireland.

Time and changing conditions affected the number of trips a rider might make in a week and how long it took him to make his run. At first, trips were scheduled only once a week, but after three months, a twice-weekly schedule was instituted. When winter weather made travel conditions more difficult, it often took fourteen days to get the mail through. In summer months, men sometimes made it in nine. For their efforts, riders were paid up to $150 a month, plus room and board—good but not extravagant wages for the time. Stage drivers over the same route made up to $300 a month, and young men who struck it rich in the silver and gold fields made many times more. Pony Ex-

press division superintendents, on the other hand, made only about $90 per month.

The rides were hard, but men who were fit and used to the hardships of western life were able to endure them. Express rider Thomas Owen King, who rode out of Fort Bridger, testified, "My longest ride was from Salt Lake City to Ham's Fork, one hundred and forty-five miles, which I covered in thirteen hours. I don't know how far I could have ridden in those days, with just time to eat a little. I don't remember that I ever felt tired."[67]

No rest was taken at relay stations either. Instead, at that point the rider had to push his stiff, weary muscles to greater effort— dismounting, transferring the *mochila*, jumping onto a fresh horse, and racing off down the trail. The rider was allowed two minutes to complete the whole process, and he repeated the changeover every ten miles between home stations. William Campbell said:

I was soon to find that "riding express" had more hard work than fun in it. We got exciting adventures at times to help keep things more interesting than plodding oxen along the dusty roads; but our work was more strenuous than freighting. It took sheer grit and endurance at times to carry the mail through.[68]

Despite the strenuousness of their jobs, many young men welcomed extra challenges. Such was the case of Howard Ransom Egan, son of district superintendent Howard Egan. Egan the younger, substituting for a regular Pony Express rider who was sick, was once heading westward at dusk in the wilds of Utah. Seeing a gleam of light ahead in the narrow canyon through which he had to pass, he advanced cautiously and discovered a band of Indians gathered around a campfire.

Fearless in the Saddle

Rather than turning back and taking a safer route, Egan lashed up his horse and galloped straight ahead. He later stated:

> Striking in the spurs and giving an awful yell, a few jumps of the pony brought me to about the middle of the camp, when my gun began to talk, though pointed up in the air, and my yells accompanied each shot. I got a glimpse of several Indians who were doing their best to make themselves scarce, not knowing but there might be a large party of whites after them. . . . Later I got it from some friendly Indians that there had been a trap set to catch an express rider for the purpose of seeing what he carried to make him travel so fast.[69]

Record Rides

Another high-spirited rider was Jack Keetley, known as the "joyous jockey of the Pony Express." On the strength of a bet, Keetley carried the mail from Big Sandy, Nebraska Territory, to Elwood, Kansas (across the river from St. Joseph), then doubled back with westbound mail that he carried to Seneca, Kansas. It was a trek of thirty-one hours, "without a stop, not taking time to eat, but eating my lunch as I rode,"[70] Keetley stated. To determine the length of the ride, division superintendent A. E. Lewis measured the distance with an odometer attached to his buggy wheel—it was 340 miles.

Keetley insisted that his ride set the record for the longest ride made by a Pony Express courier, but other riders claimed to have made equal or longer runs. A ride by Pony Bob Haslam during the Paiute War in the summer of 1860 not only rivaled Keetley's for distance, but stood as being one of the most harrowing on record since he had to evade hostile Indians. Haslam's ride was broken by rest periods, however. A ride by Pony Express rider William Cody—later to become known as "Buffalo Bill"—might have been slightly longer than Keetley's, but the great showman did not claim to have made such a record run until much later in his life, when his reputation for stretching and embellishing the truth was well known.

While Keetley, Haslam, and Cody compete for the honor of longest ride, men who pushed themselves and their horses to make the fastest rides are just as deserving of notice. The names of most are not recorded, but the few identified participants expressed pride and satisfaction at being a part of an effort that demanded the cooperation of all concerned.

The first such ride occurred as civil war loomed on the horizon in 1860. News of the election of President Lincoln was vital to the nation, and it was carried by Pony Express messengers from St. Joseph to the telegraph station at Fort Churchill, Nevada, in about seven days, a record for speed at the time. Lincoln's inaugural message of March 4, 1861—carried by Pony Express messengers from the telegraph at Fort Kearny to Fort Churchill—did not travel as quickly due to inclement weather. Snowdrifts clogged mountain passes; icy wind and snow knifed across the plains. Nevertheless, horsemen covered sixteen hundred miles in the shortest time possible—twelve days. (The period of seven days is erroneously reported by many historians.) Two horses were ridden to death in the course of the colossal effort to get the mail through. One rider, W. A. (Bill) Cates, who carried the message across Wyoming, later remembered:

> It was tough going. The message got a good start out of Kearney [sic], but the

broke the routine, and made every Pony Express rider feel that he was helping to make history."[72]

Asleep in the Saddle

Despite their toughness, even the most stalwart riders grew weary sometimes. Joaquin Miller, who rode ponies over another mail route in the Northwest, described the efforts he made to stay awake during his rides. "I became tired, then sleepy—oh, so sleepy! I pinched myself, sang old California songs, gave the Modoc war-whoop, told whopping big lies to keep myself awake, but almost tumbled from my horse dozens of times that long, long night."[73] Undoubtedly many Pony Express riders resorted to similar techniques as they fought sleepiness on their runs.

Rider Thomas King told the story of how, after riding eighty miles at night, he came to a relay station without having passed Henry Worley, another Pony Express rider scheduled to be traveling in the opposite direction. Worley reported that he had missed seeing King on the trail that night as well. Yet station keepers testified that both men had come through on time. King remembered, "We had both been so sound asleep in our saddles that we did not know when we passed each other."[74]

Leisure Time

Not only did Pony Express couriers have to deal with the exhaustion and stress of long rides, but they had to cope with too much free time. Most did not ride more than four times a week. Even after catching up on lost sleep, hours and days of spare time needed to be filled.

Showman Buffalo Bill Cody claimed to have made the longest Pony Express ride.

closer it got to the mountains, the worse the conditions got. We had the best horses available—several of them were killed—and, considering what we had to fight, the record was the most wonderful ever made by the Pony Express."[71]

Another rapid transit relay involved carrying the news that Fort Sumter had been fired on in April 1861. The event marked the beginning of the Civil War. William Campbell said of such rides, "Such things

If they were near civilization, that task was relatively easy. Their careers made them glamorous and popular with everyone, particularly young women, and they could spend their days going on picnics, going out to dinner, attending parties, or taking part in any other entertainment that suited their fancy. Riders out of St. Joseph lived in the luxury of Patee House between runs, and when these occurred only once a week, they might enjoy six days of unbroken leisure. When a twice-weekly schedule went into effect in the summer of 1860, layovers were shorter with less time for fun and relaxation.

In cities and communities farther west, riders were treated as heroes as well. Dances and parties were thrown in their honor. Good-hearted farm women prepared home-cooked meals for them. Young girls competed for their attention, and even though hard-working riders were weary, they often had enough energy left for flirtations. Thomas King remembered that after a 200-mile-ride to Salt Lake City, he would call on his girlfriend and take her for a walk on his free evenings.

On stations far from cities and towns, life could be boring, however. Men passed the time at their home stations by playing cards, sleeping, reading, and helping the station tender with chores. Undoubtedly conversation was a popular pastime. William Campbell remembered a friendly soul he encountered at one station:

The telegraph had been extended to Fort Kearney [*sic*], and often I had to wait for

Facsimile of a letter carried by the Pony Express, containing the news of Abraham Lincoln's election.

Beloved by the Ladies

John Frye, one of the most charming of Pony Express riders, was a favorite with many of the young ladies he passed on his route. Legends grew up around his name, and authors Raymond and Mary Lund Settle recount two of them in *Saddles and Spurs: the Pony Express Saga*.

"A charming story is told of how the young women would wait for him along the trail with cakes, cookies, and other culinary dainties. These he snatched from their hands on the run and ate them as he galloped along. They noticed that he had trouble with the cookies, for he could hold them with only one hand. The other was required to manage his horse. It occurred to them that if they made them with a hole in the center he could stick them upon his fingers and get along nicely. Thus was born the well-known doughnut.

An equally charming one concerns the making of a 'Log Cabin' quilt. Frye wore a red necktie which the young lady seamstress wished very much to sew into the article. Frye, however, liked the tie himself and would not give it up. Consequently she resorted to a bit of strategy. Next time he was due to come along, she mounted a horse and rode down the trail to meet him. When he came by she fell in beside him and again asked for the tie.

In a spirit of mischief Frye put spurs to his horse and dashed ahead. Not to be outdone she applied the quirt [riding whip] to her horse and soon overtook him. She made a grab for the tie, missed it, and got hold of his shirt tail. A piece of it tore off. With great glee she carried it home and sewed it into the quilt where she had planned to put the tie."

---

big news that was coming in, or that was expected. . . . The telegraph operator at the fort was a good fellow, and always had a supply of cookies on hand. He would say: "Sit down here, Billy, and eat some cookies and wait a little while longer. There's more news scheduled to come in over the wire." Well, I had my own schedule to maintain, but I had things figured out pretty well and knew just where I could save time on the run; so I would wait till the very last minute.[75]

Couriers sometimes took responsibility for getting their own meals. Most knew how to "juggle a frying pan," and some aspired to real cooking. The story of Pony Bob's wager that he could bake a pie became legendary after he followed through on his bet but mistakenly used sulfur as one of the ingredients. The pie was such a sensation that the phrase "As yellow as a Pony Express rider's pie!"[76] was heard the length of the trail for many years.

Express rider Elijah "Uncle Nick" Wilson told about Pony Express riders and station attendants who livened up the monotony by playing practical jokes on one another—putting salt in the coffee or prickly pears in a bunk, or hiding a sleeping man's trousers. One rider found a prairie dog hidden in his blankets. "They had about as much deviltry in them as high-school boys have nowadays; played about the same sort of tricks, only ours were more of the rough-and-tumble sort, in keepin' with the times,"[77] he explained.

New riders were often the butt of jokes. Wilson remembered one incident in which he and a friend went about frightening a "tenderfoot" by telling tales of life in the wild. "We began to turn the talk of some of the bloody happenings along the trail. We didn't spare the color as we went on with stories of the massacrin' of emigrants and the murderin' of miners, and the ambushin' and killin' of riders and station hands,"[78] he recounted.

The two men finished by rigging up a sheet as a ghost and frightening both the newcomer and an Express rider coming into the station. Pete, the incoming rider, reacted by shooting the sheet full of holes, and the newcomer refused to ride the next leg of the trail. Wilson ended the story: "Bob had to take the mail through that night to help pay for the trick. We had to pay for the sheeting, too, that Pete's bullets had riddled. As for the tenderfoot, he was off before daybreak back to his home town. He never showed up on the line again."[79]

Backdrops for Adventure

Stations were frequently the setting for Pony Express adventures. The two hundred or more men who operated them—particularly those in Wyoming, Utah, and Nevada—were vulnerable to weather, outlaws, Indians, and any other threat common to the frontier in the 1860s. They coped with stresses and responsibilities that would have demoralized most ordinary men. Raymond and Mary Lund Settle observe, "The station keepers and stock tenders were fully aware of the [precariousness of the] situation, yet they calmly settled themselves down in the isolated, practically defenseless little stations along the route."[80] Most received little recognition or acclaim for their work, but the success of the great experiment would have been impossible without their determination.

Way Stations on the Trail

Stations where riders could rest and where exhausted horses could be exchanged for fresh ones were essential to the Pony Express enterprise. By the time the venture was well under way, about 190 such rest stops, ten to twenty miles apart, were spaced across the country.

An accurate, all-inclusive list of these stops does not exist due to lost or incomplete records, changes in the route, and changes in the names and locations of some stations. Many sites, however, have been identified.

Some are marked by buildings still in use; some are nothing more than rough remains. Others have entirely disappeared or are distinguished only by historical monuments, unpretentious reminders of relay points along the trail.

Home and Relay Stations

Two types of stations served Pony Express riders. One was the home station, the point

Simpson Springs Station in Utah served as a rest stop for riders. Here, tired horses were swapped for fresh ones.

where horsemen began and ended their rides. Home stations offered relatively complete accommodations, since riders might eat and sleep there for several days.

Home stations often housed large numbers of horses, extra supplies, and two to four stockmen to care for animals and do routine chores. Hay was sometimes raised on home stations, both for use there and to send to smaller relay stations. Tenders usually had the equipment and expertise to perform tasks such as shoeing horses and repairing damaged tack. The former in particular was a task that was not always easy due to the spirited nature of the animals involved. Levi Hensel, who worked for the Pony Express, remembered:

> I had the contract to shoe the Overland Stage and Pony Express horses that ran from Kennekuk to Big Sandy. . . . The animals that John Frye and Jim Beatley used to ride were the worst imps of Satan in the business. The only way that I could master them was to throw them and get a rope around each foot, stake them out, and have a man on the head and another on the body, while I trimmed the hoofs and nailed on the shoes. They would squeal and bite all the time I was working with them. It generally took half a day to shoe one of them.[81]

Relay or "swing" stations were spots where a rider paused to change his tired horse for a fresh one during the course of a run. Relay stations were usually more austere, staffed by a keeper and perhaps a stockman or two. Accommodations for humans were often the simplest at these locales, but there were stables and corrals for the horses used on that leg of the relay. Most relay stations relied on food and supplies shipped by wagon from nearby home stations.

Some of the Best

Stations varied widely in size, layout, and quality of accommodations. Some were lone structures such as the simple one-story building at Thirty-two Mile Creek in Nebraska. According to Sir Richard Burton, who broke his stage journey there, "The station-master was the head of a neat-handed and thrifty family from Vermont; the rooms, such as they were, looked cozy and clean, and the chickens and peaches were plump and well 'fixed.'"[82]

Some stations were comfortable homesteads, which were numerous on the eastern end of the trail. A farm or ranch family often welcomed the chance to make extra money by boarding riders and caring for Express company livestock. At Guittard's homestead, a clump of wooden buildings set on the edge of a shady, wooded creek in Kansas, "the ham and eggs, the hot rolls and coffee, were fresh and good,"[83] according to Burton, who was usually critical of station accommodations. Guittard's was only a relay station for Pony Express riders, however, so presumably they never had a chance to fully enjoy the benefits of the good cooking offered there.

Some stations were located at hotels or hostelries in towns where a rider could enjoy the luxury of a good bed between runs. The Seneca Station in Kansas was set in a small community that boasted a two-story hotel run by a landlady named Mrs. Smith, who set a splendid table and offered dances and other entertainment. Expressman Frank Root writes, "[She] was a model landlady, and no one ever stopped there and partook of a meal without hoping he might some day come again."[84]

In Salt Lake City, Pony Express riders were housed in a two-story hotel called the

An attendant stands in the huge stable doorway of the Pony Express Museum in St. Joseph, Missouri.

Salt Lake House, which had a ballroom and a sitting room. It was the best of its kind in town, although it attracted "a rough-looking crowd of drivers, drivers' friends, and idlers, almost every man openly armed with revolver and bowie-knife,"[85] according to Burton.

Sportsman's Hall, on the western slope of the Sierra Nevadas, was a spacious inn and Pony Express station that offered riders and other guests good food, hospitality, and comfort despite its isolated locale. The hall could house up to a hundred guests. "A huge stable sheltered their horses, while an am-

ple, smelly cauldron of boiling lye in the yard at the rear gave olfactory assurance that there would be sufficient soap to wash away the dust and grime of travel,"[86] one author notes.

Rough Accommodations

Many stations were far less comfortable, clean, and welcoming. Some, particularly those in the West, had been quickly built and were rough-and-ready structures, sitting by themselves in the middle of dreary wastelands or in isolated treeless canyons. Buildings were often cobbled together of stones, adobe, or rough boards and provided the barest essentials a rider needed. At least one, a relay station at Dugway, Utah, was, according to one observer, "a mere 'dug-out'—a hole four foot deep, roofed over with split cedar trunks, and provided with a rude adobe chimney."[87]

Most of these facilities had dirt floors, no window glass (if they had windows), and some, like the one at Cold Springs, Nevada, were open to the stars. Burton describes that station as "a wretched place, half built and wholly unroofed; the four boys, an exceedingly rough set, ate standing. . . . We slept . . . under the haystack, and heard the loud howling of the wolves, which are said to be larger on these hills than elsewhere."[88]

Few of these crude stations were heated except perhaps by a cooking fire, which filled the air with smoke. Most were small and sparsely furnished with boxes and rough boards for tables and chairs. A traveler wryly describes his experience with one makeshift bench: "Our only seat was a kind of trestled plank, which suggested a certain obsolete military punishment called riding on a rail."[89]

Sleeping arrangements were usually casual. Beds were often narrow, hard bunks built into the wall. Sometimes men slept on the dirt floor or on cots that were infested with bedbugs and fleas. Burton describes bedding down at the Cottonwood Springs Station in Nebraska (not to be confused with the Cottonwood or Hollenberg's Station farther east in the state): "We entered the foul tenement, threw ourselves upon the mattresses, averaging three to each, and ten in a small room, every door, window, and cranny

Roughing It

With a keen eye and straightforward style, renown author Mark Twain gives his first impressions of the simple adobe stations that served stage passengers and Pony Express riders on the plains. Twain wrote of his experiences traveling west in his personal narrative, *Roughing It*.

"The station buildings were long, low huts . . . the roofs, which had no slant to them worth speaking of, were thatched and then sodded or covered with a thick layer of earth, and from this sprung a pretty rank growth of weeds and grass. It was the first time we had ever seen a man's front yard on top of his house. The buildings consisted of barns, stable room for twelve or fifteen horses and a hut for an eating room for passengers. This latter had bunks in it for the station keeper and a hostler or two. You could rest your elbow on its eaves, and you had to bend in order to get in at the door. In place of a window there was a square hole about large enough for a man to crawl through, but this had no glass in it. There was no flooring, but the ground was packed hard. There was no stove, but the fireplace served. There was no shelves, no cupboards, no closets. In a corner stood an open sack of flour, and nestling against its base were a couple of black and venerable tin coffeepots, a tin tea pot, a little bag of salt and a side of bacon. . . . The table was a greasy board on stilts, and the table-cloth and napkins had not come—and they were not looking for them either."

being shut . . . and despite musquetoes [mosquitoes], slept."[90]

Such conditions may not have offended some tough Pony riders, but more particular ones may have chosen to take their blanket out under the stars for the night.

Beans and "Wolf Mutton"

Food on the trail was often poorly cooked, greasy, covered with flies, perhaps even spoiled due to a lack of refrigeration. At all but exceptional stations, it was simple and limited in variety. Cured meat such as ham, bacon, and tripe (the stomach lining of cattle) was a staple, although keepers enjoyed fresh meat when they could get it. This might have included buffalo or pronghorn antelope.

Dried fruits and beans were basics of the diet, and most station keepers kept stocks of molasses, pickles, flour, cornmeal, tea, and coffee on hand. Baked goods such as bread had to be prepared and, with station keepers in charge of the kitchen, sometimes made no appearance at the table. Meals were often simply an easy-to-prepare dish such as stew or beans. Burton refers to a dinner he ate at Ruby Valley, Nevada, where the stationmaster, a Colonel Rogers, was also an Indian agent: "We dined in the colonel's stone hut . . . After us, [Chief] Chokop and five followers sat down with knife and fork before a huge tureen of soft pie, amongst which they did terrible execution champing and chewing with the noisiness of wild beasts, and eating each enough for three able bodied sailors."[91]

When supplies ran low due to floods or winter snow, or when an Indian attack made procuring supplies too dangerous, station keepers went hungry or made do with what they could find. One traveler at the time observed that their "diet is sometimes reduced to 'wolf mutton' [coyote] or a little boiled wheat or rye; and the drink to brackish water; a pound of tea comes occasionally, but the droughty souls are always out of whisky and tobacco."[92] Despite such Spartan rations, station keepers often shared what little they had with Indians, either to win their friendship or because some tribes were destitute, trying to survive on government reservations.

Stocking the Essentials

Food supplies were not the only necessities that had to be brought in regularly to stock relay stations. Most stations had been set up in accordance with how far a horse could run, so they were not always in the most practical of locations. Hay, grain, and even water were unavailable at some sites. All essentials had to be hauled in from the nearest town or home station, sometimes at enormous labor and expense.

In addition to food and water, equipment such as spare bridles, ropes, brushes, currycombs, horse liniment, and manure forks were kept on hand at every station so that expensive animals could be groomed and kept in fine shape. Screws, hinges, putty, wagon grease, and twine were stocked for making repairs. So were tools and housekeeping materials such as axes, hammers, saws, brooms, buckets, candles, tin dishes, matches, scissors, needles, and thread. All were vital for the everyday routine. Every station keeper also maintained a supply of crude medicine such as castor oil, cream of tartar, and turpentine in case of illness, and for winter he had blankets and buffalo robes to help ward off the cold.

A rider changes horses at a relay station. Accommodations varied significantly from station to station.

Life on the Station

The lifestyles of station attendants varied according to their character and the locale of their station. Those who lived near civilization often enjoyed all the comforts common to the era. They could visit friends, attend church on Sunday, and take part in social activities that a community at that time would offer, always keeping in mind that they had to be on hand to receive a Pony Express rider when he came through.

On out-of-town posts, life was quieter and entertainment rare. Even on unsettled stretches of trail, however, a fair number of travelers broke their journey at the stations. Pony Express riders, stagecoaches, wagon trains heading west, and wayfarers on horseback passed back and forth each week, and stations were logical places to pause, water horses, purchase a meal, and even spend the night. For attendants who were comfortable with solitude, the trail undoubtedly seemed as busy as a modern highway appears to us today.

Some station attendants were so antisocial that they were sullen and unwelcoming even to the occasional passerby. For instance, the landlady at Midway Station refused to serve stage passengers a meal when she was not given warning that they were arriving. At

Carson Sink Station, the surly stationmaster met his guests armed with a revolver and refused to provide them with either water, firewood, or food.

In other cases, visitors were warmly welcomed, and a keeper's hospitality and talkativeness were signs of how isolation had its effect. Burton found stationmaster J. A. "Doc" Faust at Rush Valley, Utah, to be ready and willing to talk, and of the stationmaster at Box Elder Creek Station in the wilds of Wyoming, he writes: "Mr. Wheeler was exceptionally civil and communicative; he lent us buffalo robes for the night, and sent us to bed after the best supper the house could afford."[93] Undoubtedly, a traveler like Burton from as far away as England was enjoyed and long remembered by sociable station keepers who passed their days far from the hustle and bustle of cities and towns.

A Keeper's Tasks

The duties of station keepers included caring for horses and maintaining the stations. A station attendant had to ensure that a fresh horse was saddled and ready to go when a Pony rider came pounding along the trail. An alert attendant kept a watchful eye out for a telltale cloud of dust, his ears attuned to the thudding of hooves, and knew to the moment when to have the horse in the yard. After the rider had gone on, keeper and stockmen attended to brushing, feeding, and watering the exhausted animal, then making sure that it was comfortably and safely stabled until it was needed again.

Station maintenance was almost as important as caring for horses. Tasks included cooking, crude carpentry, tending crops, repairing broken equipment, and nursing sick

A Squalid Scene

Many stations doubled as stagecoach and Pony Express stops along the trail, but this did not always mean that they were clean and comfortable establishments. In *The City of the Saints and Across the Rocky Mountains to California*, explorer and English author Sir Richard Burton gives a critical appraisal of Ham's Fork, a squalid station in Wyoming run by a Mormon man with two wives. Polygamy was a practice accepted by the Church of Jesus Christ of Latter-day Saints in the 1800s.

"At midday we reached Ham's fork, the northeastern influent of Green River, and there we found a station. . . . The station was kept by an Irishman and a Scotchman— 'Dawvid [David] Lewis:' it was a disgrace; the squalor and filth were worse almost than the two—Cold Springs and Rock Creek— which we called our horrors, and which had always seemed to be the *ne plus ultra* [the worst] of Western discomfort. The shanty was made of dry stone piled up against a dwarf cliff to save back wall, and ignored doors and windows. The flies . . . darkened the table and covered every thing put upon it; the furniture, which mainly consisted of the different parts of wagons, was broken, and all in disorder; the walls were impure, the floor filthy. The reason was at once apparent. Two Irishwomen, sisters, were married to Mr. Dawvid and the house was full of 'childer,' [children], the noisiest and most rampageous of their kind. I could hardly look upon the scene without disgust."

animals and men. At stations that were stagecoach outposts, keepers were expected to offer food and lodging to passengers when they arrived. In a few stations, attendants had to put the finishing touches on buildings and surroundings that had been hurriedly constructed at the beginning of the project.

For taking such responsibility, Russell, Majors & Waddell paid each man between $50 and $100 a month. Chapman writes:

During the summer of 1860, the company spent a great deal of money putting the route in readiness for winter. The tents and makeshift shacks with which the relay attendants were compelled to put up during the opening weeks of the service, were replaced with better buildings. Wherever it was possible hay was raised for the ponies, thus cutting down the company's enormous outlay for feed. The

Station keepers were on the lookout for incoming riders who stopped only long enough to change mounts.

Prosperous and Popular

Some Pony Express stations were farms or ranches, and the best of these were prosperous, popular establishments run by well-respected men like George Hollenberg. In his book *Pony Express—The Great Gamble*, author Roy Bloss gives Hollenberg's life history and describes his station, located in Kansas.

"The [Pony Express] company was . . . fortunate in its appointment, by Superintendent A. E. Lewis, of an agent at Cottonwood Creek, two miles northeast of present-day Hanover, Kansas. . . . He was George H. Hollenberg, a native of Hannover, Germany, who after a series of youthful mining adventures in California, Australia and Peru, and in a shipwreck off the Florida coast, was advised by a doctor to go West.

About 1857, with his wife, Sophia, he enterprisingly selected a site on the Oregon trail that, with equal benefit, would serve as home, trading post and public hostelry. Hollenberg's substantial cabin, built on a slight rise of the ground, and his long stable nearby, attracted trade from overland emigrants, stage passengers, teamsters, and traveling military forces. The Hollenberg Station, as it is sometimes called, boasted a bar for thirsty travelers and provided an abundant table for its hungry guests. The owner deservedly prospered and hired clerks for his store, one of whom became postmaster at the station."

The Hollenberg Pony Express Station (pictured) reportedly provided good hearty meals and comfortable accommodations.

station keepers and their helpers put in much of their time working on new quarters and putting up hay.[94]

At times a station attendant was called on to ride the trail himself, and even put his life on the line in so doing. J. G. Kelley was assistant stationmaster at Sand Springs in May 1860 when the regular rider came into the station dying from an Indian bullet. Kelley was the lightest man at the station and was commandeered to carry the *mochila* down the trail. On his return, he escaped an Indian ambush only by spurring his horse at top speed through a grove of trees.

William Streeper, who carried supplies to the stations and worked as a station keeper in Utah for a time in the summer of 1860, remembered that he acted as a substitute rider one day when the regular man was drunk. Majors prohibited alcoholic beverages, but a few riders became intoxicated anyway and were unable to perform their duties. "Most of the pony riders and the station keepers I knew respected the pledge they had to take; but naturally there were a few who didn't,"[95] Streeper recalled.

Trouble on the Station

Life at the stations could be monotonous or a wild and dangerous adventure. Terrible storms lashed the premises in winter; floods or heavy snowfall could leave tenants isolated with only a bare minimum of supplies. Outlaws and Indians prowled the trail, and most keepers were too far from civilization to be able to summon aid if necessary. Horse thieves were another threat, and station tenders had to be constantly on alert to ensure that their charges were not driven off. One author writes, "The fine stock at the Pony Express stations was guarded night and day. Without redoubled precautions under such circumstances, the 'Pony' riders would soon have been afoot."[96]

At times, station attendants themselves were the source of trouble. Many were rough-mannered, independent individuals who were quick to fight, and firearms were always on hand to settle a dispute. Two or three men, cooped up on a remote station for weeks on end, could drive each other to violence, as one writer observes: "During the winter months, when there was little to do but wait for the arrival of the next 'Pony,' there were natural disagreements and a few attempted killings. Men, thrown together in such lonely surroundings, are quite apt to rasp each other's nerves."[97]

Sometime in late 1860, H. Trumbo, keeper at Smith's Creek Station in Nevada, became involved in an argument with Montgomery Maze, a Pony Express rider who had formerly been a station keeper at Sand Springs. Trumbo reportedly discharged a pistol at Maze several times (apparently without harming him), and Maze retaliated by shooting Trumbo. Trumbo was seriously wounded in the hip, and Maze became a candidate for discharge without pay for violating his pledge not to quarrel or fight with any other employee of the firm.

On July 12, 1861, stock tender James Butler Hickok shot and killed station agent David McCanles and two other men at Rock Creek Station near the Nebraska-Kansas line. The deaths, reportedly sparked by an argument, marked the beginning of "Wild Bill's" gunslinging career. Many have debated whether or not the young stock tender murdered the three men in cold blood, but an inscription on the back of a photo of McCanles, written by an employee of Wells, Fargo & Company, seems to exonerate Hickok. It reads:

> Portrait of McCandless [*sic*] on horseback, a desperate character who, with two

others, was shot dead at this station . . . by our stock tender. It was done in self defense. Seven of these men attacked our stock tender, and he had to cope alone against them, but succeeded in killing three and putting the rest to flight. He was brought to trial, but was soon honorably acquitted.[98]

"Casual Heroism"

Just as station attendants sometimes shot first and asked questions later, riders occasionally used their guns in order to stay alive and carry out their responsibilities. There were numerous hazards to be met and overcome on the trail, but many horsemen seemed almost fearless when faced with danger. Author David Nevin writes of the young adventurers, "The sense of invincible self-confidence and devotion to duty . . . was affirmed by dozens of his fellows in hundred[s] of acts of casual heroism in the face of floods, snowstorms, buffalo stampedes, and Indian attacks."[99] The riders' motto was "The mail must go through." There were few exceptions to the rule.

CHAPTER 5

"The Mail Must Go Through!"

Pony riders faced endless dangers and difficulties as they worked for the Pony Express. They galloped across terrain that was slippery mud in winter and choking dust in summer, alive with flies and mosquitoes, home to wild animals and hostile Native American tribes. They forded treacherous rivers and struggled over rugged snow-covered mountains.

Traveling at night with only the moon and the stars to light their path, they had to maintain a sharp lookout and rely on the instincts of their horses to keep them on the trail. Some men were thrown off and broke bones. Some were wounded. Some rode when they were sick. Those who coped with illness and injury did so miles from the nearest doctor and had to rely on the crude first aid skills of the station keeper to keep them in the saddle.

At least five Pony Express couriers died while carrying out their duties. In April 1860 the *New York Tribune* reported that one man, traveling at high speed at night, was killed when his horse "stumbled over an ox lying in the road, throwing the rider, and the horse fell upon him."[100] The following July, according to the *San Francisco Daily Evening Bulletin*, a rider drowned while crossing the Platte River. A month later, a riderless horse arrived at a station in western Nevada. Its

As some Pony Express riders left the station they wondered if they would live to return.

rider was never found and was presumed dead. At least one rider died of his wounds after being attacked by Indians. Another lost his way on the trail and froze to death near Fort Kearny in December 1860.

The vast majority of riders, however, successfully completed their runs, thrilling the nation, who saw them as men of uncommon valor, heroes straight out of a storybook. One newspaper of the time expressed that admiration:

> The loud peals of thunder, and the fierce flashes of lightning, or even the falling of the drenching rain, detains him not. . . . Whether sundried or soaked, snow-covered or frozen, by day or by night, in starlight or darkness, be he lonely or merry, forward he hastens, until the thrice-welcome station is just there, in sight, when he leaps from his saddle, and with full heart rejoices that his task for the present is fully accomplished. . . . He rides all alone, over prairies and mountains, whether up hill or down, on rough ground or smooth, among true friends or foes, he hies [travels] swiftly on, until in the shadowy distance the relay is seen, and his duty's performed.[101]

"The Lonesomest Kind of Job"

Despite national admiration and a feeling of accomplishment, the Pony riders sometimes felt lonely and cut off from society. Prairies and deserts were boundless and for vast distances empty of human life. Nights on the road were black and silent except for coyote howls and the thudding of the pony's hoofs. Riders put in hours of riding with only their own thoughts for company. "It was the lonesomest kind of a job,"[102] recalled Charles Cliff, who was one of the riders from St. Joseph to Seneca.

Only one or two men rode each section of trail, so few had the chance to get to know other riders. Undoubtedly all heard of the exploits of men like Pony Bob Haslam and Jack Keetley, but familiarity was limited to stories passed by word of mouth along the trail. Few riders got within miles of such legendary characters, and never got to talk to them. "The only other rider I ever really knew was George Town, who took the mail from me at Seneca, when I had pounded out my eighty or eighty-five miles from St. Joe,"[103] Cliff remembered.

Even at the stations, riders had little chance to talk with or make friends with anyone. Changeovers at relay stops were never more than two minutes long, and conversations with attendants were usually limited to practical topics like horses and weather. "Look out for this black [horse] today—he's shore [sure] on the prod [excitable]," a keeper might remark, or, "The crick's [creek's] up a foot—better hit the ford a little high."[104] When asked a question about the latest news in the East, a rider often had time only to wordlessly toss a newspaper into an attendant's hands as he spurred away down the trail.

Afraid to Ride

The image of the Pony rider was one of bravery, but most couriers knew the meaning of fear, and some were not as heroic as the public perceived. Traveling alone, lightly armed, in all kinds of weather and at all times of the day and night, most were aware that they were extremely vulnerable to a variety of dangers. Some wondered each time they went out if they would survive the ride, or live to see family and friends again. At times their fears grew so overwhelming that they refused to leave the safety of the station.

The threat of Indian attack was the most powerful incentive not to ride, as Henry Avis discovered on one of his relays. On a day in 1861, traveling west of Fort Laramie, Wyoming, Avis reached his home station—Horseshoe Station—with the expectation of handing the *mochila* to his replacement. That rider, however, had heard of a possible attack by a war party of Sioux and refused to take to the trail. Judging that the job was more crucial than the danger, Avis pushed on with the mail to the next home station to the west.

Conditions were bad throughout the area, however, and the return rider at that station admitted that he, too, was afraid to ride. Ignoring his own fears, Avis turned back to Horseshoe, which he was fortunate to reach without incident. Because he had completed over 220 miles of riding under dangerous circumstances, he was rewarded by his supervisor with a handsome bonus of $300.

"Supermen of the Saddle"

In addition to the strain of loneliness and fear, riders coped with physical stresses related to their work. A courier might make a run only twice a week, but his time in the saddle was long and exhausting. Distance between home stations was commonly about a hundred miles, and speeds averaged about eight miles per hour (top speeds were about

Often, dangers such as the threat of Indian attack prevented even the bravest rider from continuing the journey.

twenty miles per hour) so rides could be as long as twelve hours. Horses were galloped whenever possible, and for a man in the saddle, that kind of jolting was grueling. Men often arrived at their destination bleeding from the nose and mouth after their runs. "As easy as it may seem to some for a man to bestride horse after horse for 140 miles, there were few men able to endure it,"[105] states one writer.

Some men rode extra relays, but this was not a common practice. Few riders, even young, physically fit ones, could maintain the pounding for longer stretches than they were normally assigned. The strain of making extended runs regularly would have been too much for a normal man to bear.

The wear and tear of such physically demanding work undoubtedly caused all kinds of health problems. Headaches, backaches, muscle cramps, and other related discomfort and distress must have plagued the riders. Many continued to ride even after they had been injured in falls or wounded by Indians, and so endured the pain and aftereffects of their injuries in addition to everyday weariness. At least one man rode for a time while suffering from a fatal illness; Alexander Carlyle died of tuberculosis after working only a few months for the Pony Express.

Many riders found the work too punishing and quit. Some lasted a few weeks, some only a few days. Only a small number endured the entire year and a half of service. Chapman writes, "The riders who withstood the grind, month in and month out, were supermen of the saddle, whose extraordinary deeds have for the most part been lost, unfortunately, in the chaos of the frontier."[106] By the end of the enterprise, experts estimate that a total of about two hundred men had ridden for the Pony Express, an indication of the high turnover rate.

Rough Road

Rough terrain caused many of the aches and pains a rider felt and contributed to accidents as well. Although prairies and deserts appeared smooth at a casual glance, they were in fact pocked with rocks and boulders, bristling with bushes and weeds, undercut by animal burrows, rugged and uneven over every square inch of their surface. Burton refers to "pitch-holes," or "chuck-holes" that made traveling over the prairie "a sore task." These were shallow gullies, sometimes ten to fifty feet in width, through which rivulets of water flowed in spring and early summer, but which lay dry the rest of the year, posing a particular threat to travelers.

Even the well-worn Oregon–California Trail that riders followed as far as Fort Bridger, Wyoming, was nothing more than ruts cut into the earth by endless wagon wheels. The ground was rough and dangerous when it came to navigating one's way, and riders needed to be alert lest their ponies make a false step and fall.

Inevitably, accidents did occur, sometimes with disastrous results, as in the case of the five fatalities. In another potentially serious incident, a rider named Sam Hall was galloping his horse along the trail in Wyoming when the animal stepped in a badger's hole. Both horse and rider were thrown, and Hall's foot became entangled in the stirrup. He was dragged two hundred yards before his boot jerked loose, and he lay for a time bleeding from his nose and mouth before he recovered enough to get to his feet. Beaten and sore, he was able to rendezvous with his horse back at the last station from which he had come.

Thomas Owen King was following a rough, narrow trail somewhere between Fort Bridger and Echo Canyon, Utah, in the spring of 1860 when his horse lost its footing

The stage line near Deep Creek Mountains still shows the thousands of ruts cut by wagon wheels. Pony Express riders often followed the road at night without the luxury of light.

and threw King and the *mochila* off. Fortunately, only the *mochila* tumbled over the edge of the cliff, and King was able to retrieve it and continue his ride. No mention is made of the bumps and bruises he must have suffered during his fall.

Richard Erastus "Ras" Egan, another son of division superintendent Howard Egan, was carrying the mail westward on a stormy night in November 1860, when his horse stepped in a hole, fell, and broke its neck. Undaunted, Egan scrambled to his feet, unhooked the *mochila* from the saddle, and covered the remaining five miles of his relay on foot. Again, no mention is made of the hurts he must have sustained when he was thrown.

Danger on All Sides

Darkness made riding a rough road even more dangerous, and many close calls occurred after nightfall. At the age of ninety, William Campbell looked back and remembered, "It wasn't always easy to keep the trail. We didn't have any of these signal lights they put up for the flyers [trains] in these days."[107]

Animals, particularly large ones, could be a danger for a galloping rider in the dark. "The greatest danger I faced on the trail was buffaloes," said Campbell. "They were along the trail in western Nebraska by thousands. If a rider ever ran in to a herd, he was gone."[108]

Campbell also recounted an incident when a pack of wolves followed him as he made his ride between stations one night:

> They were big ones . . . about the size of a Newfoundland dog. When I dashed past them, they took after me. I happened not to have my revolver—had lent it to another boy that day. The station was several miles away, and they were getting too close for comfort. Finally I thought of my horn, and blew it as loud as I could. The pack drew back a little way; then they began to come on. I blew the horn again. . . . After checking them in this way for a number of times, I finally made it to the station.[109]

Added to the danger posed by darkness and wild animals were the weather conditions faced by Pony Express riders. Exposed to the elements day and night and in every season, the men had to be hardened to everything from bone-chilling wind and cold of high mountain passes to grilling desert heat that sapped a man's energy. "The air was like the breath of a furnace," author Burton writes, describing August weather in Wyoming. "The sun was a blaze of fire—accounting, by-the-by, for the fact

Buffalo were some of the many threats to Pony Express riders on the trail.

that the human nose in these parts seems invariably to become cherry-red."[110]

Sunburn was a comparatively minor discomfort, however. Pony riders rode in blinding dust storms that scoured their skin and filled their eyes, nose, and mouth with sand and grit. They picked their way through dense fog and across icy expanses where a false step might send them tumbling over a precipice. They endured pounding hail and sleet, and downpours of rain that drenched and chilled them. They struggled through rivers made hazardous by floods, quicksand, and dangerous currents.

The first near drowning occurred early in the Pony Express experience—on the first ride. As the unidentified rider plunged into the rain-swollen Platte River near Julesburg, Colorado, his horse was knocked off its feet and swept downstream. Thinking quickly, the courier snatched the *mochila* and abandoned his mount. He swam to shore, resourcefully borrowed a fresh horse from a passerby, and continued his ride. The original horse was rescued and later returned to the closest station.

"The Toughest Treatment"

Blizzards and snowstorms were common on the prairies as well as in the mountains. Warren Upson's battle across the Sierra Nevadas was only the first of dozens of severe struggles that riders made through snow and storm. Rider Richard Cleve was caught in a blizzard after leaving Midway Station, Nebraska, one night. The snow was so thick and deep that he lost track of the trail. He described his efforts to survive: "I would get off the horse and look for the road, find it and mount the horse, but in five yards I would lose it again. I tried it several times, but gave it up, so I dismounted

and led the horse back and forth until daylight."[111] The mail went through, although Cleve spent thirty-six hours trying to complete his relay.

Storms were one of the afflictions of William Campbell's life when he rode in Nebraska. "Sometimes the fierce wind and rain that came on that level country would slow us up a good deal. It was the blizzards, though, that gave us the toughest treatment,"[112] he remembered. Caught in one snowstorm, Campbell kept to the trail by keeping track of the top of tall weeds during the day, and trusting to the instinct of his horse at night.

William Frederick Fisher told of a January storm as he set out from Rush Valley for Salt Lake City in 1861. "Wind and blindin' desert dust at first, then snow. It was about the fiercest blizzard I ever faced,"[113] he recalled. He had difficulty finding his relay stations and almost collided with a Russell, Majors & Waddell wagon train that had camped on the trail to wait out the storm. The wagon boss urged him to stay in camp and weather the storm in safety, but Fisher insisted on continuing his ride.

Eventually he "got himself into a tangle of troubles," becoming hopelessly lost. With few options, he huddled down with only his horse and a snowbank for protection and waited.

> As I sat there holding the reins, I began to get drowsy. That snow bank looked like a feather bed, I guess; and I was just about to topple over on to it and take a good nap when suddenly something jumped on to my legs and scared me. I looked up just in time to see a jack-rabbit jumping away through the snow.[114]

Realizing that many a man had frozen to death after falling asleep in the snow, Fisher

Travelers across the prairies experienced all types of weather from baking sun to blizzards, and Pony Express riders did not have even the protection of a stagecoach or covered wagon as they faced such exposure. In *The City of the Saints*, Richard Burton describes one common weather phenomenon—a fast-rising thunderstorm that he saw while crossing through Kansas in 1859.

"Beyond Walnut Creek, a dense nimbus [cloud], rising ghost-like from the northern horizon, furnished us with a spectacle of those perilous prairie storms which make the prudent lay aside their revolvers and disembarrass themselves of their cartridges.

Gusts of raw, cold, and violent wind from the west whizzed overhead, thunder crashed and rattled closer and closer, and vivid lightning, flashing out of the murky depths around, made earth and air one blaze of living fire. Then the rain began to patter ominously upon the carriages; the canvas, however, by swelling, did its duty in becoming water-tight, and we rode out the storm dry. Those learned in the weather predicted a succession of such outbursts, but the prophecy was not fulfilled. The thermometer fell about 6 degrees (F.), and a strong north wind set in, blowing dust or gravel, a fair specimen of 'Kansas gales,' which are equally common in Nebraska, especially during the month of October."

credited the rabbit for saving his life. He scrambled to his feet, mounted up, and let his horse find its own way. The two eventually made it to the safety of a farmhouse, where Fisher was given breakfast and thawed his frozen hands and feet.

His adventure did not end there, however. The storm continued to blow, but Fisher believed in the company motto that "the mail must go through." He set off again, only to get lost a second time. Eventually he stumbled into a settlement and took shelter at another farmhouse. When the storm broke and the stars came out, he continued his ride. "They [the stars] looked cold as icicles, but I didn't mind that," he remembered. "I could see my way now, so I went on again round the point of the mountain to Port Rockwell's station. They give me a fresh horse there and I struck out for Salt Lake on the jump."[115] Fisher successfully made it to Salt Lake City, finishing his ride

at four o'clock in the morning, well behind schedule but glad to be alive.

Random Shots

While weather created predictable hazards on the trail, events sometimes cropped up that were as dangerous as they were unanticipated. William Campbell remembered the case of a fierce bulldog that lived at a ranch that he passed on his run. The dog would sometimes run out snarling and snapping, spooking his horse, and making a pest of itself.

One night I thought I would scare this animal. I fired my pistol in his general direction, but my aim was a little too good, for I killed him. The station tenders told me the next day that the rancher had threatened to shoot the next Pony Express rider

Pony Express couriers encountered all kinds of difficulties on their rides; some even faced the occasional temptation. In Howard Driggs's *The Pony Express Goes Through*, rider William Campbell recalls how he coped with such challenges.

"Those blizzards were about the worst things we had to face. When we would come into stations through them, we generally jumped off and grabbed up a few cookies and a cup of hot coffee to thaw us out a bit for the next freezing stretch; then off we would go again. . . .

Frequently someone would offer me a drink of whisky to 'warm me up,' but I never took it. I'd given my word I wouldn't. Besides, my religious parents had brought me up with a feeling that the stuff wasn't good for a fellow. . . .

I remember getting plum lost one dark night along the Platte River. A thunderstorm had made things black as ink for a time. I could hear the river running close by, but couldn't see which way it was going; so I took my lariat, which I always carried for emergencies, and tossed one end of it into the stream. I could tell from the way it pulled the direction the water was flowing. That helped me get my bearings. It wasn't always easy to keep the trail."

---

who passed. The regular trail led between his house and a barn on the ranch, but there was a branch road outside. Thereafter I took the branch.[116]

J. G. Kelley, a veteran who survived all kinds of hazards on the trail, recalled passing a wagon train one day and being suddenly broadsided by a hail of bullets. "What I consider my most narrow escape from death was being shot at by a lot of fool emigrants, who, when I took them to task about it on my return trip, excused themselves by saying, 'We though you was an Indian.'"[117]

Outlaws

Pony riders did not commonly have trouble with outlaws and other lawbreakers while on their runs, but occasionally they coped with this kind of danger. Some men such as rider Melville Baughn were an equal match for the outlaws they faced. When Baughn, who rode the trail near Fort Kearny, Nebraska, found that he had been the victim of a horse thief, he took matters into his own hands. Few details are available to flesh out the story, but William Lightfoot Visscher writes, "Baughn followed the thief to Loup Creek, secured his pony, and rode back to Kearney where he found the mail pouch and finished his trip, a little behind schedule time."[118] The means—sly and stealthy or openly forceful—that Baughn used to take back his horse are left to the reader's imagination. Baughn must have been a tough, no-nonsense type of man, however, who was not intimidated by lawlessness or by the law. A few years after the Pony Express ended, he was hung in Seneca, Kansas, for murder.

Often station attendants were the ones who faced outlaws, whether western bad men or criminals who had fled the East for greener pastures. At times a keeper simply ran afoul of a rough individual whose temper or personality made him a menace to all who crossed his path. Such was the case for station keeper Hod Russell near Fort Laramie, Wyoming, in the summer of 1861.

Russell had been playing poker with a hunter named Bob Jennings, a six foot two giant with a sullen disposition and a bad reputation in the area. Jennings lost at the game, and he took the loss badly. The next day, just after Russell finished helping a Pony rider spur off into the distance, a bullet out of some nearby bushes dropped the attendant in his tracks.

Stagecoach passengers who happened to witness the attack agreed that Jennings was the killer. A posse was formed and a neighborhood scout, "Buffalo Bill" Comstock, was called in to help track Jennings down. Comstock successfully located and captured the hunter, who was taken back to Fort Laramie and speedily hung. According to one writer, the next day the "Pony Express rider who galloped up to the station at Fort Laramie . . . knew, by something which swung against the sky, that one more frontier crime had been expiated [atoned for]."[119]

"Buffalo Bill" Cody

William Cody, who began working as a Pony rider sometime in the spring of 1860, seemed to have had more encounters with outlaws than any other Pony Express man on the trail. Whether accounts of his adventures are true or merely part of the legend that grew up around his name, no one can tell.

One story goes that Cody, only fourteen at the time, was stopped one day by an outlaw. Author William Lightfoot Visscher recounts the story:

"You are a mighty little feller to be takin' such chances as this."

"I'm as big as any other feller," said Cody.

"How do you make that out?" the highwayman asked.

"Well, you see Colonel Colt has done it," the youngster replied, presenting at the same time a man's size revolver of the pattern that was so prevalent and useful among the men of the frontier. "And I can shoot as hard as if I was Gin'ral [Stonewall] Jackson," he added.[120]

Apparently respecting the young rider's spirit and weapon, the outlaw allowed Cody to depart.

In another instance, Cody was entrusted with a large sum of money in addition to the mail. Learning in some mysterious way that bandits were in the area, he hid the money and *mochila* in a saddle blanket. He then substituted a second pair of saddle pouches that he hung in plain sight. As expected, the outlaws stopped Cody on his ride and threatened his life unless he gave up the money. Cody flung the substitute pouches at the head of one bandit, fired a bullet at the other, and urged his horse forward, knocking the first man down. A contemporary of Cody's recounted, "The fallen man, though hurt, scrambled to his feet as soon as he could, picked up his rifle, and fired after the retreating youth, but without effect, and young Cody rode on, arriving at the station on time, and reported what had happened."[121]

On a third occasion, while between rides in Wyoming a few months later, Cody stumbled upon a hideout of murderous horse thieves while bear hunting. He managed to shoot one and gave the others the slip. Having lost his horse, the Pony rider walked twenty-five miles to the nearest station. He arrived safely, and the next morning still had strength

Life was dangerous at a Pony Express station, but at least in one case, cold-blooded murder brought prompt retribution. Robert Spotsworth, who succeeded Jack Slade as division superintendent, gives a firsthand account of the capture and subsequent hanging of Bob Jennings, who shot attendant "Hod" Russell near Fort Laramie in 1861. Spotsworth's account is included in Arthur Chapman's *The Pony Express*.

"They [the posse] flung themselves on Jennings, and soon had him bound and helpless, though he put up a hard fight. Then, putting Jennings astride one of his own horses, and binding his feet underneath, they took him to the nearest station on the trail, where they were lucky enough to catch a west-bound stage. The passengers aboard marveled at the ways of the West when they saw Jennings bound to the rear boot of the stage with heavy chains. Not satisfied with that, Jennings' captors buckled him with stout straps. Then they rode behind the stage as an escort until the fort was reached and Jennings was delivered to the commandant.

The hanging that followed was entirely unofficial, but it was surprisingly quick. Stage employees and others along the trail, who had gathered on hearing that Russell's slayer had been captured, assisted in the execution, which had its unique features.

Jennings, without even being blindfolded, was led to an immense pole . . . which was used for hoisting fresh meat in the air, to keep it away from flies and wild animals.

It was his body, swinging from the end of the pole, which attracted the attention of the next Pony Express courier to arrive, in the early morning hours."

to join the posse that set out to track down the outlaws.

Indian Trouble

Many of Cody's experiences in the Pony Express relate to outlaws, but an equal number revolve around Indian attacks as well. William Russell's great experiment took place during a tumultuous time in western history, when the lives of riders and station attendants alike were put at risk by hostilities with Native American tribes. The months of May through July 1860 were particularly dangerous ones for the Pony Express. As author Roy Bloss points out, members of the Paiute tribe, angry at the white man's invasion of their territory, "forced an abrupt halt to the pounding hooves, even before the shuttling Pony had time to live up to the glowing promises of the nation's impulsive press."[122]

The Paiute War

Of all the dangers faced by Pony Express riders and station attendants, Indian attack was the most constant and grave. More than two-thirds of the route ran across land inhabited by Native American tribes. West of Salt Lake City, the track cut squarely across hunting grounds of the Paiute (pronounced Pi-yute) and Shoshone tribes, whose hatred and distrust of the white man had grown increasingly intense. Pony rider George Washington "Wash" Perkins, who rode the trail in Utah, remembered, "The Injuns were lurkin' all along the trail, trying to get us. We could see their smoke signals on the hills. It was a pretty dangerous gauntlet to run; but we skirted round every ambush point the best we could, to keep out of range of their arrows and bullets."[123]

Strained Relations

Traditionally, relations between Native Americans and whites on the frontier were strained

Indians posed the most constant threat to lone Pony Express riders.

but not always hostile. Early trappers and mountain men had respected the Native American way of life and left their food supply undisturbed. Some had even adopted native customs and married native women. As time passed, however, hunters, explorers, and settlers became disrespectful of the traditions and lifestyles of the tribes with which they came in contact. They took over land, killed and scared off game, even attacked and killed people for no good reason. For instance, in 1832 Joe Meek, a member of a trapping party from the East, killed a Shoshone "as a hint to keep the Indians from stealing our traps." When asked if the victim had stolen any, Meek replied, "No, but he looked as if he was going to."[124]

Despite such insensitivity, Plains tribes such as the Sioux, Crow, and some Shoshones were generally peacefully disposed toward settlers. Not until whites began serious violations that included breaking treaties and killing off buffalo in record numbers in the late 1800s did they become increasingly hostile. "The Indians were pretty quiet on my run while the overland service was going," remembered William Cates, who rode on a central part of the route. "A good many of them couldn't 'savvy' [understand] the idea of a lone rider pelting across the country at such a speed, with no particular object in view."[125]

Nevertheless, tensions were high in places, and not all riders were as fortunate as Cates. Shortly after Pony Express runs began, Alexander Carlyle, who rode out of St. Joseph, was shot at by an Indian along the trail. So straight was the attacker's aim that Carlyle's hat was knocked from his head, and he never again wore any kind of head covering while in the saddle.

Many a Pony rider learned after a time that if he encountered Indians, he only had to raise his rifle to determine if they were hostile or not. A hunting or scouting party would generally ride away if they were not looking for trouble. Other riders believed in taking a bolder approach—they would charge straight through the midst of a gathering of Indians, catching them off guard before they had time to attack. If the warriors did not give chase, all was well and good. If they did, the grain-fed horses supplied by Russell, Majors & Waddell were able to outrun Indian ponies and carry a rider to safety.

First Strike

On the western end of the Pony Express trail, tensions ran higher than in the East. An incident on the second run out of St. Joseph, which began on April 13, 1860, gave a forecast of coming events. When the westward-bound mail reached Nevada, it was held up for six hours at Roberts Creek after Paiutes drove off all the horses at the station there. Newspapers downplayed the mishap, however, and riders completed the trip in just over ten days despite the interruption.

There was good reason for Native American resentment in the West. The winter of 1859–60 was severe in Nevada, and the 6,000-member Paiute tribe suffered intensely from hunger and cold. Hundreds of prospectors, looking to strike it rich in the Nevada hills where silver had been discovered, made matters worse. They invaded Paiute hunting grounds and killed and scared away game. Piñon trees, whose nuts were an important food for the Paiutes, were cut down for firewood. The additional appearance of Pony Express riders shuttling back and forth along the trail seemed to emphasize the white man's assumption that he owned the land.

About a month into the Pony Express experiment, resentment erupted into full-blown hostilities. No one can be sure exactly what

Settlers who cut down trees and killed game provoked the anger of some Indian tribes in the West.

triggered the blowup, but Pony rider Elijah Wilson gave this explanation:

> They [the Indians] didn't take kindly to the white men's rushing over their country, killing their game and settling on some of their choicest homelands. It took only a reckless act on the part of some whites to start them on the warpath. Such an act came out there one day when a fool took a shot at an inoffensive old Indian who was up on the hillside trying to trap some ground squirrels to feed his family. The Indian was killed and left lying there beside the trail. The killer had something to brag about; but it was the boys that ran the Pony Express and other innocent folk that had to foot the bill for this and like atrocities.[126]

Angry and impatient, the Paiutes held a council at Pyramid Lake in late April to determine how to respond. All but one of the leaders of the council wanted war. Even Chief Winnemucca, who had been friendly to white settlers in the past, believed that an attempt to drive away the newcomers was justified.

Present at the council was a young warrior named Moguannoga, who was eager to fight. At some point he left the council with a small band of warriors and attacked the Williams Pony Express Station in Nevada. The motive for the strike was never determined. Some believe that Moguannoga attacked without

Not all Paiutes wanted to go to war in the spring of 1860. At least one young warrior, Numaga, understood the cost of fighting against white intruders, and he counseled for restraint and compromise rather than bloodshed. Author Roy S. Bloss details Numaga's efforts to avert war in *Pony Express—The Great Gamble*.

"Of that branch of the tribe living on the reservation an Indian named Numaga was the chosen chief. White men called him 'Young Winnemucca,' the war chief, but he was not. . . . Numaga was an Indian statesman, intellectual, eloquent and courageous, an impressive figure standing six feet tall, with a Roman nose and broad chin and firm mouth, marking a character of strong will and decision. He had lived among the whites in California, could speak English, and was well aware of the numerical and material superiority of the race against whom his people would unleash the arrow. In the closing days of April he rode from camp to camp, from family to family, and from friend to friend, urging and beseeching them to decide against war.

At last, in May, all the chiefs of the tribe sat in council. Numaga remained silent, waiting to the last, listening and weighing the arguments. When all had spoken he arose and began an impassioned plea to avert bloodshed and to find the way to peace.

At this moment of eloquence there dashed up to the council an Indian on a foam-flecked pony. Moguannoga, the rider declared, with nine braves, had burned Williams Station on the Carson River the previous night, and killed four whites.

All the steam and passion faded from Numaga. Sadly he turned to the chiefs and counseled against further talk. It was now time to prepare for war; surely, the soldiers would come to fight."

provocation. Others believe the story was more complicated. They claim that in early May 1860, while Pony Express station keeper J. O. Williams was camping upriver, his two brothers, David and Oscar, captured a Paiute woman, held her prisoner, and abused her. After trying to rescue his wife, her husband appealed to Moguannoga for help.

No one can say for sure which account is the most accurate, but the result was the same. On May 7 Moguannoga and his party of warriors rode to the station and killed David and Oscar Williams. Two other men who were staying at the station—Samuel Sullivan and an individual known only as Dutch Phil—were also killed. The opening blow had been struck, and the Paiute War had begun.

War!

After burning the station to the ground, Moguannoga and his men headed west, bound for Buckland's Station. Changing their minds as they rode, they instead drove off a few head of cattle from a ranch they passed, then returned to Pyramid Lake to report their actions to Winnemucca. The news of the successful attack was enough to push the council to action, and all able-bodied Paiutes prepared for an offensive against the enemy.

While they made ready, a Pony courier from the east discovered the destruction of Williams Station and carried the news to Carson City. Messengers were sent far and wide to warn prospectors and settlers of danger. At the same time, a band of a hundred volunteers, led by army major William O. Ormsby, set out for Pyramid Lake to avenge the deaths.

The expedition was little more than a disorganized spree—Ormsby's men were careless, poorly armed, and had underestimated the skills of their opponents. Approaching Pyramid Lake, they unwittingly rode into a trap set by the Paiutes. Twenty-six of the volunteers were killed in the ensuing fight, and as they retreated, twenty more were cut down. A wounded Ormsby tried to surrender and was also killed, his body tossed into a ravine. The battle of Pyramid Lake went down as one of the most tragic misadventures of frontier history.

News of the catastrophe reached Buckland's Station on May 15, when survivors of the battle straggled home. As the word of this and attacks on other stations and ranches spread, the people of the Carson River Valley reacted to protect themselves. The Penrod Hotel at Carson City was turned into a fortress. In Virginia City, women and children were evacuated from their homes to an unfinished stone building that could withstand an assault. The citizens of Silver City built fortifications on a hill outside the town and erected imitation cannons there in hopes of intimidating any approaching Paiutes. Isaac Roop, provisional governor of newly formed Nevada Territory, immediately notified California authorities and asked for aid.

His appeal was answered almost immediately. Volunteers from California towns such as Downieville, Sacramento, Placerville, San Juan, and Nevada City were soon on the road. By the end of May, about eight hundred men had gathered at Carson City, ready to fight. Two hundred were U.S. Army troops sent out of San Francisco, where they had been stationed.

Again, a band of volunteers marched toward Pyramid Lake. Again, the Paiutes were waiting. On June 3 a three-hour battle took place, and this time the volunteers were able to rout their opponents. Twenty-five Indians were killed and the rest were driven north. After a short pursuit, the volunteers decided that further bloodshed was not in anyone's best interest. They returned to Carson City and disbanded, while government agents attempted to bring a semblance of peace back to the region. With the help of a friendly Paiute chief named Numaga, a measure of order was restored. Paiute raids continued for many months, however, evidence that hostile feelings continued on the part of many frustrated Native Americans.

Real Grit

During the months of May and June 1860, Pony Express stations across Nevada lay unprotected and exposed to Indian attack. The attendants at Cold Creek Station were driven out, the Roberts Creek Station was destroyed, and the attendant at Dry Creek was killed.

William Streeper, substitute Pony Express rider and carrier of "mule mail" in Nevada, was one of the few brave men who dared cross the desert during the early days of June. He discovered the station burned and the keeper killed at Simpson's Park, and was one of the first to come upon Dry Creek and find the mutilated body of Ralph Rosier (or Lozier), the station keeper there. "When I opened the door my hair just stood up on end. They say it won't do it, but I tell you mine did. There lay the murdered and scalped keeper, stark naked,"[127] Streeper remembered long after.

Indians had attacked early one morning, killing Rosier and wounding an attendant, John Applegate. When Applegate, who was

This inscription on a rock in Nevada commemorates two station keepers killed in the line of duty.

suffering terribly, asked for a gun, attendant Lafayette "Bolly" Bolwinkle gave it to him, thinking that he wanted it to defend himself. Applegate promptly shot himself in the head, putting himself out of his misery.

Bolwinkle and trading post owner Si McCandless then decided to make a desperate run for the next station. They managed to elude pursuing Paiutes and cover the twelve miles to safety, although Bolwinkle, who had not had time to pull on his boots, was disabled for some time after that with severely cut and bruised feet. "We hear a lot of praise for the boys that rode the ponies, and they deserve it," stated rider George Perkins, "but I'm not forgettin' the boys that took care of the stations and the stock. It took real grit to stay with that job, always exposed to Injun arrows. Far more keepers than riders lost their lives or were wounded in the Pony Express service."[128]

Staying alive was a special challenge for station keepers during those tumultuous days. Early in June Peter Neece, the station keeper at Willow Creek, was approached by several Indians, who demanded something to eat. He offered them a twenty-four-pound sack of flour, but when they indicated that they wanted a sack apiece, Neece refused and ordered them to leave. In retaliation, they shot one of Neece's cows. Neece responded by drawing his revolver and killing two of the intruders.

After dark the raiding party returned with reinforcements. Neece was ready. He, his station attendant, and Elijah Wilson, who happened to be at the station, positioned themselves in the sagebrush surrounding the building. As the Indians approached, the men created confusion by repeatedly firing out of the darkness, then leaping to one side and firing again. The Indians saw flashes of light and gun reports from the desert, but finding no one at the station, they rode away in frustration. Years later Wilson admitted that he had done little more than jump from spot to spot. He gave all the credit for the standoff to Neece. "We had confidence in Pete. He was the bravest fellow I ever knew—clear-headed, too, and a dead shot."[129]

Riders in Peril

Stations in Nevada were particularly vulnerable to Indian attack during the summer of 1860, but Pony Express riders had many close calls and near-death experiences as they rode up and down the trail. At least one rider, an unidentified Hispanic, was shot by Indians while carrying the mail across Nevada in the middle of the Paiute War. The injured man made it into the next station, but then collapsed and died.

While riding for the Pony Express in Wyoming, William Cody had several encounters with Indians. One occurred about eight miles away from Horse Creek Station, where a party of fifteen warriors ambushed him in a canyon. Only his straight shooting and his superior horse got him out of the tight situation and away to safety. He writes in his autobiography, "My mount was a California roan pony, the fastest in the stables. I dug the spurs into his sides, and, lying flat on his back, I kept straight on for Sweetwater Bridge eleven miles distant. A turn back to Horse Creek might have brought me more speedily to shelter, but I did not dare risk it."[130]

Many of Cody's experiences were later exaggerated to dramatize his already exciting life. Undoubtedly, other Pony Express riders' experiences grew more dramatic in the telling over the years as well. Some seem almost too unbelievable to be true. Nevertheless, they capture the real courage demonstrated by many riders, and the depth of the danger some faced while riding the trail.

Joseph Barney Wintle had several encounters with Indians as he rode between Fort Kearny and Cottonwood Springs in Nebraska. Once he was chased for miles but outran the attacking party at the cost of his horse's life. Twice he came unexpectedly upon Indian encampments but escaped unhurt; first by dismounting and pretending to adjust his saddle girth; a second time, by handing off his horse to a nearby warrior, then coolly entering a lodge. What he did inside is unknown, but when he came out, he gave the warrior a small present. In both cases, he then remounted and proceeded on his way, unhindered by anyone. Since Wintle's encounters were farther east, perhaps he was dealing with tribes who were less aggressive than the Paiutes and Shoshones in the West. District Superintendent Major Howard Egan, who rode as a substitute for regular Pony riders, was once chased by several Paiutes who were waiting for him on a lonely portion of the trail in Utah. Drawing his revolver and firing in all directions, Egan was able to spur past them. When they gave chase, he outdistanced them. According to reports, one of the attacking party later told Egan that his bold action had convinced them that a backup escort was following him not far down the trail.

During the height of the tension in the West, William F. Fisher and George Perkins were traveling as a team eastward from Ruby Valley, Nevada, when they were attacked by Indians who were waiting for them as they passed a blind spot on the trail. Fisher was nearly killed by a bullet that went through his hat, while Perkins found an arrow lodged in the *mochila* he was carrying.

A Race for Life

The following account of an episode in Buffalo Bill Cody's Pony Express days, related by a station agent and included in William Lightfoot Visscher's *A Thrilling and Truthful History of the Pony Express*, demonstrates the sensationalism that colored many tales of the great showman's life. At the age of fifteen, Cody exhibits almost unbelievable dexterity as he outshoots and outruns the leader of a hostile band of Indians.

"With set teeth, flashing eyes, and determined to do or die, Will Cody rode on in the race for life. . . . The chief, whose fleet horse was bringing him on at a terrible pace, [was] threatening to reach there at the same time with the pony rider.

Nearer and nearer the two drew toward the path, the horse of Cody slightly ahead, and the young rider knew that a death struggle was at hand. He did not check his horse, but kept his eyes alternately upon the pass and the chief. The other Indians he did not then take into consideration. . . .

When the chief saw that he would come out of the race some thirty yards behind his foe, he seized his bow and quick as a flash had fitted an arrow for its deadly flight. But in that instant, Cody had also acted, and a revolver had sprung from his belt and a report followed the touching of the trigger. A wild yell burst from the lips of the chief, and he clutched madly at the air, reeled, and fell from his saddle, rolling over like a ball as he struck the ground.

The death cry of the chief was echoed by the braves coming on down the valley, and a shower of arrows was sent after the fugitive pony rider. An arrow slightly wounded his horse, but the others did no damage, and in another second Cody had dashed into the pass well ahead of his foes. It was a hot chase from then on until the pony rider came within sight of the next station, when the Indians drew off and Cody dashed in on time, and in another minute was away on his next run."

Although friendly with the Indians in this photograph, Buffalo Bill Cody told stories of life-threatening shootouts with Native Americans.

Pony Bob's Record Ride

Pony Bob Haslam had to outrun Indians several times while riding his route. On one March trip, he finished his run with his jaw broken by an arrow and his arm shattered by bullets. His most famous exploit, however, was the ride he made at the outbreak of the Paiute War, when Native American emotions were running high, and danger along the trail was acute.

Shortly after the attack on Williams Station, Haslam galloped out of Friday's Station, prepared to make his usual seventy-five-mile ride to Buckland's in the East. He learned of the outbreak of violence on his arrival at the station at Carson City. There, the volunteers had taken all the horses, leaving him with no fresh mount. Pausing to feed and water the one he had, he hurried on. At Buckland's, a fresh horse awaited, but the replacement rider refused to set out on the next leg of the relay because of the Indian threat.

Offered a $50 bonus by the station keeper if he would carry the mail farther, Pony Bob unhesitatingly replied, "I will go at once,"[131] and set out. Keeping up the pace and changing horses at Sand Springs and Cold Springs Stations, he made it to the next home station at Smith's Creek—a total of one hundred ninety miles away from Friday's. There, he handed off the mail to the next rider and proceeded to catch a few hours rest after his extended run.

Less than nine hours later, however, the westbound mail came through and Haslam gamely set off westward, retracing his prior journey. This time he encountered tragedy at Cold Springs. Indians had raided the station, killed the keeper, and run off the horses. Terrified but determined, Haslam kept to the saddle and urged his tired horse on. He remembered:

It was growing dark, and my road lay through heavy sage brush, high enough in some places to conceal a horse. I kept a bright lookout, and closely watched every motion of my poor pony's ears, which is a signal for danger in an Indian country. I was prepared for a fight, but the stillness of the night and the howling of the wolves and coyotes made cold chills run through me at times; but I reached Sand Springs in safety and reported what had happened.[132]

At Sand Springs, Haslam persuaded the frightened station keeper to accompany him west to safety. Farther down the road, at the relay station at Carson Sink, the two men found fifteen survivors of the Pyramid Lake battle, barricaded against possible attack. Haslam changed horses and rode on, finally finishing his relay at Friday's Station. By then he had been in the saddle thirty-six hours with only a short rest. He had covered 380 miles and was only three-and-a-half hours behind schedule. The ride went down in the record books as one of the longest made in Pony Express history. Haslam was awarded $100 for his performance.

Helping the Pony

Alarmed that Pony Express men were being killed and stock and supplies destroyed, William Finney, the Pony Express agent in San Francisco, requested the commander of the army in California to post at least seventy-five soldiers at stations along the line to discourage further violence. His request was refused.

Finney then set out to get a firsthand view of the situation. In Carson City around the end of May, he reluctantly decided that riders should not make their runs until stations were rebuilt and resupplied, and until the route was made more secure. Telegraphing a postponement of mail deliveries until further notice, Finney appealed to those who had a stake in the Pony Express—merchants in Sacramento—to raise the money needed to secure and rebuild the route. (Significantly, he did not turn to Russell, Majors & Waddell, a sign of the tight financial situation the company was in at the time.) On June 6 Finney requested:

> Will Sacramento help the Pony in its difficulty? We have conferred some benefits, have asked but little, and perhaps the people will assist. Can anything be done in your city towards paying expenses to furnish arms and provisions for 25 men to go through with me to Salt Lake to take and bring on the Express? . . . What is wanted is $1,000 for the pay of the men, $500 for provisions, and 20 Sharpe's rifles. . . . I will guarantee to keep the Pony alive a little longer.[133]

Generously, Sacramentans responded by raising almost $1,500. San Franciscans promised to help as well. Prompt assistance allowed Finney to organize a work party of twenty men and purchase provisions and horses for the ruined stations. Finney fell ill at the last minute and had to hand over leadership of the party to division superintendent Bolivar Roberts, but Roberts was fully up to the task.

On June 9 he and the work party set out to repair the damage that had been done. They constructed stations that were more secure, and left five men at each to protect the reconstruction. Working their way across the desert, they also carried eastbound Express mail that had not gone out of Sacramento since May 25.

On June 16 Roberts rendezvoused with division superintendent Howard Egan at Roberts Creek Station, and the two parties exchanged greetings and mail. Egan was carrying three hundred pieces of westbound mail that had accumulated in Salt Lake City since the beginning of Indian hostilities. (Pony riders had continued to make their runs between St. Joseph and Salt Lake during May and June.) Egan was escorted by a detachment of U.S. troops from Camp Floyd near Salt Lake City, and the soldiers obligingly gave Roberts and his party a safe escort back to Carson City.

They arrived there on June 22, and the mail was carried on to San Francisco. It arrived on June 25. The Pony Express, out of service in the West for about four weeks, was back in business. For some time thereafter, however, deliveries were erratic and riders made their runs across the Nevada–Utah desert escorted by government troops, averaging a mere forty miles a day. It was the middle of July before anything like a regular schedule was observed again.

Lingering Trouble

The Paiute War had officially ended, the Pony Express line was rebuilt and fortified, and officials assured the public that the fleet delivery service was once again functioning normally. To emphasize its capabilities, William Russell announced that twice-weekly runs would be instituted beginning about July 1. Some time would pass before such an ambitious schedule could be regularly followed, however, and Pony Express station keepers and riders coped with Indian attacks for several months after the initial hostilities had been dampened.

In September 1860 Elijah Wilson took part in a skirmish with several Indians who

"Something Should Be Done!"

The following editorial, taken from *San Francisco's Daily Evening Bulletin*, describes conditions in Nevada that threatened the future of the Pony Express in May 1860. Indignation felt by Californians when they learned that protection from the army in California was not forthcoming is apparent in the article.

"W. W. Finney, the agent of the Pony Express, called upon us this morning and gave us some sad news respecting the perilous condition of that enterprise, which already has taken such deep root in the fancy of the people. He had just received telegraphic dispatches from Carson City, which state that the station at Simpson Park was burned on Monday last, and that it is supposed to have been the work of the Indians; that the station-keeper and all the animals are yet missing. . . . The dispatch further informs Mr. Finney that the man who came in with the last express from Reese river, was forced, by fear of the Indians, to lie by for thirty-six hours at the Smith Creek Station . . . and that though the express, leaving here on the 18th, had duly started on the perilous journey, there was doubt as to who would be the succeeding expressman, with the letters which left here yesterday.

Upon the reception of this news, Mr. Finney called upon Gen. Clarke [with the army in California] to ascertain if the Government would not furnish some protection to the route. . . . Gen. Clarke, in reply to Mr. Finney's application, expressed great regret that he could do nothing. . . . Under these circumstances, Mr. Finney is fearful that the Express will have to be stopped. . . . We cannot pretend to know Gen. Clark's business as well as he does, but it seems to us that 75 men might well be spared . . . for the duty of protecting the express route. . . . In view of the exigency of the case, something should be done, and that right speedily."

were attempting to drive off Pony Express horses from the Spring Valley Station. As Wilson pursued the thieves, they shot at him, and an arrow struck him in the forehead two inches above his eye. He fell to the ground, unconscious. When two attendants pulled him to safety and tried to remove the arrow, the shaft came loose, leaving the arrowhead embedded in the wound.

Certain that Wilson was dying, the attendants left him under a tree and set off to a neighboring station to report the attack. Returning the next day, they found the rider still alive. A doctor was called in, and the arrowhead was removed. Wilson hovered on the brink of death for more than a week but finally showed signs of recovery. "In a few weeks I was riding the Pony Express again," he later recalled, "but I have had terrible headaches at different times all my life from the wound made by that flint-headed arrow."[134] For the rest of his life, Wilson wore a hat tilted over his left eye to hide the ugly scar that remained.

In another incident, station attendants Albert Armstrong and Henry Woodville Wilson were eating breakfast at the Egan Canyon Station in early October when a large war party attacked. The two men fought until their ammunition ran out, then were overwhelmed by the raiders, who broke down the door and took them captive.

After eating all the supplies in the station, the Indians took their two prisoners outside, tied them to a wagon tongue, and piled sagebrush around them. Their intention was to burn the two men alive. "A massive petrifying fear settled over Armstrong and Wilson as they abjectly gave up all hope of somehow evading a horrible, gruesome death," one author recounts. "Then, miraculously, they heard a rush of pounding hooves from the direction of a nearby hill. That welcome sound could mean only one thing—rescue."[135] Fortunately, a party of soldiers on their way to Salt Lake City arrived at the most opportune moment and was able to stop the killing. In the ensuing fight, eighteen Indians were killed. The two station men were saved.

The High Cost of War

The Paiute War and ensuing Indian hostilities proved a serious handicap to the success

This 1873 photograph shows a Paiute Indian poised to fire his rifle.

of the Pony Express. Runs were interrupted for four weeks, causing critics to belittle the Pony's reliability. They prophesied that service would come to a standstill again when winter closed the roads and mountain passes.

Seven relay stations were destroyed. One hundred fifty valuable horses were lost. Sixteen employees were killed. The cost of replacing stock and supplies amounted to at least $75,000. That total was a heavy blow for Russell, Majors & Waddell. The mighty company was on the very brink of bankruptcy and had been absorbing losses incurred by the Pony Express from the start.

Neither Indian troubles nor lack of money was the final blow to the daring experiment, however. Instead, its end came as the result of a much-anticipated technological advance, one that linked East with West better than any horseman could do. David Nevin explains: "By the end of 1861, telegraph wires had spanned the continent, and with the suddenness of a rider reining in for a change of mounts, the Pony Express era came to a halt."[136]

"Farewell, Pony!"

The Pony Express was one of the fastest means of communication in 1860, but it could not compete in speed with the telegraph, invented by Samuel F. Morse in 1837. By 1860 Hiram Sibley's Western Union Telegraph Company connected the principal cities of the East, and the Missouri & Western Telegraph Company had extended lines from the Missouri River to Fort Kearny. In the West, the Alta Telegraph Company provided service to Californians, and the Placerville & St. Joseph Overland Telegraph Company extended across the Sierra Nevadas to Carson City, Nevada.

Private telegraph companies served Americans on both coasts, but a communication gap existed in the center of the country. Successful runs by Pony Express riders proved that the central route was feasible for communication purposes and increased the demand for even better, speedier communication with the West. Author Howard Driggs writes, "The hoof-beats of the wiry little horses speeding the mail east and west simply accelerated the desire for messages clicked off with 'dots and dashes.'"[137]

Two months after the Pony Express started, Congress passed a bill to subsidize the company that would build a transcontinental telegraph system. In October 1860 Hiram Sibley won the bid to begin construction, and the route was laid out, roughly following the Pony Express trail. To speed construction, Sibley chose to begin building from both ends of the established service network—Fort Kearny and Carson City. The first poles were put in the ground near Fort Kearny in July 1861.

Pony Express riders, carrying mail along the route, kept work crews informed of one another's progress. During construction, riders continued to carry mail between Sacramento and St. Joseph, but telegrams they once carried between Fort Kearny and Carson City now only needed to be carried between the ends of the telegraph lines, a distance that grew progressively shorter as the summer passed.

In late October the two construction crews reached Salt Lake City, and the wires were joined, linking east and west. Because the country was fighting the Civil War at that time, one of the first messages to flash over the line was a confirmation of California's loyalty to the Union:

> To Abraham Lincoln, President of the United States. . . . The people of California desire to congratulate you upon the completion of the great work. They believe that it will be the means of strengthening the attachment which binds both the East and the West to the Union, and they desire in this—the first message across the continent—to express their loyalty to the Union and their determination to stand by its Government on this its day of its trial. . . . Stephen J. Field, Chief Justice of California.[138]

The Pony Fades Away

The new transcontinental telegraph service was widely celebrated, but it marked the end of the Pony Express's glory days. Important messages could be sent from coast to coast in almost split-second time, and the Express now seemed antiquated and slow. A ten-day lag in war news was intolerable when Californians could get the results of momentous battles just hours after they occurred.

Overland mail service continued, of course, because there was still plenty of business that could not be handled entirely by wire. But William Russell's involvement in the Indian bond scandal prejudiced Congress against him when he applied for a new $1 million mail contract in 1861. Instead, Congress directed that Butterfield's Overland Mail (taken over by Wells, Fargo & Company in March 1860) move its operations northward to the central route. Together it and the COC&PP Express were told to share the subsidy. That amount was not enough to get Russell's shaky business affairs back on their feet or to support the Pony Express.

In January 1861 the firm of Russell, Majors & Waddell went bankrupt, and later that year the COC&PP Express was virtually taken over by freight operator Ben Holladay. (Holladay officially purchased the company in 1862.) He and Wells Fargo continued to run the Pony Express for a time, and riders continued to make their rides, carrying the mail

A Great Change

Completion of the transcontinental telegraph marked the end of the Pony Express. Next came the need to dismantle the system that had worked so efficiently for nineteen months. In his book *The Pony Express*, Arthur Chapman provides a glimpse of that termination process and what it meant for the men involved.

"Along the familiar trail, covered by the last rider, a great change had taken place. . . . All along Slade's division—at Julesburg, Mud Springs, Fort Laramie, Horseshoe, Deer Creek, Three Crossings and Rocky Ridge, there were telegraph operators. They were scattered on the trail. . . . From San Francisco to the Missouri there was not a hundred-mile stretch without its telegraph station and its man in charge. . . .

Orders had come through to sell the horses or to add them to the livestock at the stage stations—the gallant ponies which had outrun the swift mustangs of pursuing Indians. It had been ordered that relay stations were to be dismantled or turned over to the telegraph company. Station keepers, stock tenders and horseshoers were ordered to find new jobs, and with them went the 'Pony' riders—the men who had made possible a mail service without equal in Christendom.

New jobs! Well, no doubt they were to be had, but what could offer any excitement equal to the mad scramble of men and horses at the relay stations? What could there be, to make up for the rhythmic swing of the racer's long stride?

New jobs! There were plenty in the young and growing West, but the Pony Express rider who hung up his saddle for the last time felt in his heart that there could be no other job in the world quite worth while."

The Wells Fargo and Company Express (pictured) shared the task with the Pony Express of transporting mail across America.

up and down the trail. Still, their days of service were numbered. The government subsidy contract of March 1861 specified that the Pony Express was to continue only until the completion of the transcontinental telegraph.

On October 26, 1861, two days after the official conclusion of the telegraph project, the announcement of the Pony's end appeared in western newspapers. The announcement was expected, but nevertheless sad news for many. Articles like the following flowery one in the *Sacramento Bee* mourned the service's passing:

> FAREWELL, PONY: . . . Farewell and forever, thou staunch, wilderness-overcoming, swift-footed messenger. . . . Rest upon your honors; be satisfied with them, your destiny has been fulfilled—a new and higher power has superseded you. . . . This is no disgrace, for flesh and blood cannot always war against the elements. Rest, then, in peace; for thou hast run thy race,

thou hast followed thy course, thou has done the work that wast given thee to do.[139]

Pony couriers continued to work for a time, completing their final relays, delivering mail that was already en route. The last rider, whose name went unnoted in history, handed in his *mochila* in San Francisco on November 20, 1861. By then the press had lost interest in the enterprise and did not even make mention of the fact.

Forgotten Men

After the Pony Express passed into history, William Russell became a forgotten man. Tainted by scandal, he failed to recoup his financial losses and lost standing in the business and social community of which he had been a part. He was eventually reduced to selling patent medicine (questionable remedies sold without a doctor's prescription) and petitioning William Waddell for $200 needed to file another petition for bankruptcy. His health failed, and he lived out his life with his daughter in St. Louis, Missouri, dying in 1872 at the age of sixty.

William Waddell's reputation also suffered after the failure of Russell, Majors & Waddell. He retained a comfortable home in Lexington, Kentucky, but faced many lawsuits. Angry creditors questioned his honesty. Old friends turned against him. He died the same year as William Russell, at the age of sixty-five.

Alexander Majors was somewhat more fortunate than his partners. He remained in the freighting business and later moved to Salt Lake City, where he furnished ties and telegraph poles to the Union Pacific Railroad during its construction of the transcontinental railroad. In 1869 he was present when the golden spike, symbolizing the completion of the project, was driven at Promontory Summit, Utah.

Domestic trouble broke up the Majors household, however, and Majors spent his later years living alone in a small cabin near Denver, Colorado. There he wrote his memoirs, entitled *Seventy Years on the Frontier*. Buffalo Bill Cody ran across him while Majors was working on the project and paid to have the finished manuscript published. Unfortunately, it was a financial failure. Majors died in 1900, at the age of eighty-six.

Fate of the Riders

When their mail-carrying responsibilities came to an end, the Pony Express riders had no choice but to find other work and explore new directions for their lives. Some chose careers that were distinguished; others pursued work that was more mundane. Some were not ready to settle down and went on to have further adventures.

Henry Avis tried gold mining for a time, then returned to Kansas City, where he lived until his death in 1927. Station keeper and

"You Served Us Well!"

As the Pony Express came to an end, Californians acknowledged their appreciation for its service to their state. The following article, printed in the California periodical *Pacific*, is an example of that acknowledgment. It is included in David Nevin's *The Expressmen*.

"A fast and faithful friend has the Pony been to our far-off state. Summer and winter, storm and shine, day and night, he has traveled like a weaver's shuttle back and forth til now his work is done. Goodbye, Pony! No proud and star-caparisoned [ornament-covered] charger in the war field has ever done so great, so true and so good a work as thine. No pampered and world-famed racer of the turf will ever win from you the proud fame of the fleet courser of the continent. You came to us with tidings that made your feet beautiful on the tops of the mountains; tidings of the world's great life, of nations rising for liberty and winning the day of battles, and nations' defeats and reverses. We have looked to you as those who wait for the morning, and how seldom did you fail us! When days were months and hours weeks, how you thrilled us out of our pain and suspense, to know the best or know the worst. You served us well!"

substitute rider "Doc" Faust studied medicine and became an outstanding physician. Richard Erastus Egan and William Frederick Fisher became bishops in the Mormon Church. Melville Baughn and William Carr were both hung for murder.

Charles Cliff, who had ridden Pony Express out of St. Joseph, took to driving an ox team in Colorado. He was shot by Indians while rounding up stock. To treat his wound, he later remembered, "I had the boys pour some turpentine into it. . . . It was pretty tough treatment, but the old days were pretty rough days and we took things as they handed them out to us."[140] Cliff later became a feed and flour merchant in St. Joseph. He died in 1924, at the age of eighty.

Pony Bob stayed on a run between Virginia City, Nevada, and Friday's Station for a time after the Pony Express ended, working as an express messenger for Wells, Fargo. Haslam later served as a deputy U.S. marshal in Salt Lake City, then moved to Chicago and worked for the Congress Hotel. There he entertained guests with stories of his adventures as a Pony Express rider. William Lightfoot Visscher, who met Haslam in 1907, writes:

> To see Mr. Haslam as he is in the conventional garb and quiet calling that are now his life, . . . [it is hard to believe] that the bland, mild mannered, and affable gentleman . . . had ever experienced the dangers, privations, and hazardous adventures that have marked the career of "Pony Bob" in blazing the western way.[141]

William Cody tried a variety of pastimes including buffalo hunting in the West, where he earned his nickname while providing meat for construction crews on the Kansas Pacific Railroad. In 1872 he went into show business and met dime novelist Ned Buntline, who glorified him in print. In 1883 he got the notion of creating a theatrical production, similar to a circus, that would showcase his western adventures. His "Wild West Show" was an instant success, and Cody traveled with it throughout the United States and Europe for almost twenty years.

John Frye enlisted in the Union army and became a scout. He was killed in one of the early engagements of the Civil War. Michael Whalen also joined the army, fought in the battles of Shiloh, Vicksburg Landing, and Corinth, then marched with Union general William Tecumseh Sherman from Atlanta to the sea. Wild Bill Hickok became a Union scout, then fought Indians with George A. Custer. After serving as a peace officer in several Kansas towns, he toured for a time with Buffalo Bill's Wild West Show. Hickok was shot to death in 1876 while playing poker in a saloon at Deadwood, South Dakota.

David Robert Jay, the youngest rider in the Pony Express, served in the Kansas Cavalry during the war, then settled down, got married, and became a stonemason. Major Howard Egan, district superintendent and one of the oldest riders, remained a rancher in Utah. William Campbell went into the freight business with his brother and was later elected a state senator in Nebraska. Celebrated as the last surviving Pony Express rider, he died in Stockton, California, in 1932, having lived to see the mail carried by pony, rail, automobile, and air.

Pony Express Legacy

The Pony Express was the predecessor of the railroads and helped tie the eastern and western United States together at a pivotal time in

The Pony Express was the predecessor to the Transcontinental Railroad which connected the East to the West in 1869.

the nation's history. Because it allowed for rapid communication, it played a significant role in keeping California in the Union during the onset of the Civil War.

Its riders carried 34,753 pieces of mail and lost only one *mochila*. Together, they made 308 runs in each direction and raced a total of 616,000 miles, a distance equivalent of more than twenty-four trips around the world. Part of a unique experiment, they shouldered positions of responsibility and difficulty that were extraordinary then and would still be seen as extraordinary in youth today. Authors Raymond and Mary Lund Settle conclude:

The young men who rode the racing ponies, mere boys in their latter teens many of them, were of a type and quality who deserve the unqualified admiration of youth the world over. They were clean, God-fearing, worthy of trust, and modest in the extreme. When the "Great Adventure" was over they slipped away, most of them into oblivion, with no thought other than that they had done their work well.[142]

The Pony Express riders remain symbols of our American heritage. They rode their gallant ponies as if the future of the growing country rested in their hands. Indeed, it did.

Notes

Introduction: An Adventurous Generation

1. Arthur Chapman, *The Pony Express: The Record of a Romantic Adventure in Business*. New York: Cooper Square Publishers, 1971, p. 308.
2. Quoted in Howard R. Driggs, *The Pony Express Goes Through: An American Saga Told by Its Heroes*. New York: J. B. Lippincott, 1935, p. 10.
3. Quoted in Chapman, *The Pony Express*, p. 32.
4. Quoted in Fred Reinfeld, *Pony Express*. New York: Macmillan, 1966, p. 19.
5. Quoted in Raymond W. and Mary Lund Settle, *Saddles and Spurs: The Pony Express Saga*. Lincoln: University of Nebraska Press, 1955, p. 21.
6. Quoted in David Nevin, *The Expressmen*. New York: Time–Life Books, 1974, p. 33.
7. Arthur E. Summerfield, *U.S. Mail: The Story of the United States Postal Service*. New York: Holt, Rinehart and Winston, 1960, p. 69.
8. Chapman, *The Pony Express*, p. 309.

Chapter 1: The Bright Idea

9. Quoted in Reinfeld, *Pony Express*, p. 47.
10. Quoted in Roy S. Bloss, *Pony Express— The Great Gamble*. Berkeley, CA: Howell-North Press, 1959, p. 15.
11. Quoted in Chapman, *The Pony Express*, p. 81.
12. Quoted in Bloss, *Pony Express*, p. 18.
13. Quoted in Chapman, *The Pony Express*, p. 249.
14. Quoted in Anthony Godfrey, *Historic Resource Study; Pony Express National Historic Trail*. United States Department of the Interior/National Park Service, 1994, p. 30.
15. Quoted in Godfrey, *Historic Resource Study*, p. 32.
16. Bloss, *Pony Express*, p. 84.
17. Quoted in Settle, *Saddles and Spurs*, p. 32.
18. Chapman, *The Pony Express*, p. 80.
19. Quoted in Settle, *Saddles and Spurs*, p. 35.
20. Chapman, *The Pony Express*, p. 163.
21. Settle, *Saddles and Spurs*, p. 128.
22. Quoted in Driggs, *The Pony Express Goes Through*, p. 91.
23. Chapman, *The Pony Express*, p. 163.
24. Quoted in LeRoy Hafen, *The Overland Mail, 1849–1869*. Cleveland: Arthur H. Clark, Co., 1926, p. 170.
25. Quoted in Bloss, *Pony Express*, p. 31.
26. Quoted in Summerfield, *U.S. Mail*, p. 68.
27. Quoted in Chapman, *The Pony Express*, p. 84.
28. Horace Greeley, *An Overland Journey from New York to San Francisco in the Summer of 1859*, New York: Knopf, 1964, pp. 38–39.
29. Quoted in Settle, *Saddles and Spurs*, p. 35.
30. "Pony Express, Nine Days from San Francisco to New York," *San Francisco-Daily Evening Bulletin*, March 17, 1860, p. 1.
31. Quoted in Bloss, *Pony Express*, p. 57.

Chapter 2: Ten Days to San Francisco

32. Quoted in Nevin, *The Expressmen*, p. 91.

33. Driggs, *The Pony Express Goes Through*, p. 41.
34. Quoted in James Monaghan, *The Overland Trail*. Indianapolis: Bobbs-Merrill, 1947, p. 366.
35. Quoted in Hafen, *The Overland Mail*, p. 172.
36. Quoted in Nevin, *The Expressmen*, p. 92.
37. Quoted in Nevin, *The Expressmen*, p. 92.
38. Quoted in Driggs, *The Pony Express Goes Through*, p. 161.
39. Quoted in William Lightfoot Visscher, *A Thrilling and Truthful History of the Pony Express or Blazing the Westward Way*. Chicago: Charles T. Powner, 1946, p. 33.
40. Richard F. Burton, *The City of the Saints and Across the Rocky Mountains to California*. Niwot: University Press of Colorado, 1990, p. 29.
41. Quoted in Bloss, *Pony Express*, p. 46.
42. Quoted in Settle, *Saddles and Spurs*, p. 61.
43. Chapman, *The Pony Express*, pp. 138–39.
44. Settle, *Saddles and Spurs*, p. 62.
45. Greeley, *An Overland Journey*, p. 84.
46. Burton, *The City of the Saints*, p. 48.
47. Burton, *The City of the Saints*, p. 454.
48. Bloss, *Pony Express*, p. 51.
49. Settle, *Saddles and Spurs*, p. 68.
50. Quoted in Hafen, *The Overland Mail*, p. 174.
51. Quoted in Bruce A. Rosenberg, *The Code of the West*. Bloomington: Indiana University Press, 1982, p. 115.
52. Mark Twain, *Roughing It*. New York: Harper & Brothers, 1959, p. 52.

Chapter 3: Fearless in the Saddle

53. Quoted in Driggs, *The Pony Express Goes Through*, p. 175.
54. Quoted in Chapman, *The Pony Express*, p. 85.
55. Quoted in Monaghan, *The Overland Trail*, p. 369.
56. Burton, *The City of the Saints*, p. 5.
57. Quoted in Chapman, *The Pony Express*, p. 228.
58. Twain, *Roughing It*, p. 53.
59. Quoted in Visscher, *A Thrilling and Truthful History*, p. 33.
60. Twain, *Roughing It*, pp. 52–53.
61. Quoted in Chapman, *The Pony Express*, pp. 216–17.
62. Quoted in Hafen, *The Overland Mail*, p. 181.
63. Quoted in Chapman, *The Pony Express*, p. 231.
64. Quoted in Chapman, *The Pony Express*, p. 228.
65. Visscher, *A Thrilling and Truthful History*, p. 26.
66. Quoted in Nevin, *The Expressmen*, p. 103.
67. Quoted in Chapman, *The Pony Express*, p. 234.
68. Quoted in Driggs, *The Pony Express Goes Through*, pp. 175–76.
69. Quoted in Hafen, *The Overland Mail*, p. 177.
70. Quoted in Visscher, *A Thrilling and Truthful History*, p. 32.
71. Quoted in Chapman, *The Pony Express*, p. 221.
72. Quoted in Chapman, *The Pony Express*, pp. 231–32.
73. Quoted in Chapman, *The Pony Express*, p. 247.
74. Quoted in Chapman, *The Pony Express*, p. 235.
75. Quoted in Chapman, *The Pony Express*, p. 229.
76. Quoted in Chapman, *The Pony Express*, p. 154.
77. Quoted in Driggs, *The Pony Express Goes Through*, p. 79.

78. Quoted in Driggs, *The Pony Express Goes Through*, p. 80.
79. Quoted in Driggs, *The Pony Express Goes Through*, p. 85.
80. Settle, *Saddles and Spurs*, p. 117.

Chapter 4: Way Stations on the Trail

81. Quoted in Visscher, *A Thrilling and Truthful History*, p. 36.
82. Burton, *The City of the Saints*, p. 38.
83. Burton, *The City of the Saints*, p. 28.
84. Frank A. Root and William Elsey Connelley, *The Overland Stage to California*. Topeka, KS: W. Y. Morgan, 1901, p. 197.
85. Burton, *The City of the Saints*, p. 201.
86. Bloss, *Pony Express*, p. 108.
87. Burton, *The City of the Saints*, p. 457.
88. Burton, *The City of the Saints*, pp. 487–88.
89. Burton, *The City of the Saints*, p. 166.
90. Burton, *The City of the Saints*, pp. 49–50.
91. Burton, *The City of the Saints*, p. 471.
92. Quoted in Godfrey, *Historic Resource Study*, p. 59.
93. Burton, *The City of the Saints*, p. 136.
94. Chapman, *The Pony Express*, p. 159.
95. Quoted in Driggs, *The Pony Express Goes Through*, p. 131.
96. Chapman, *The Pony Express*, pp. 157–58.
97. Chapman, *The Pony Express*, p. 160.
98. Quoted in Chapman, *The Pony Express*, p. 173.
99. Nevin, *The Expressmen*, p. 102.

Chapter 5: "The Mail Must Go Through!"

100. Quoted in Godfrey, *Historic Resource Study*, p. 62.
101. Quoted in Rosenberg, *The Code of the West*, p. 128.
102. Quoted in Chapman, *The Pony Express*, p. 216.
103. Quoted in Chapman, *The Pony Express*, p. 216.
104. Quoted in Chapman, *The Pony Express*, p. 152.
105. Visscher, *A Thrilling and Truthful History*, p. 39.
106. Chapman, *The Pony Express*, p. 214.
107. Quoted in Driggs, *The Pony Express Goes Through*, p. 179.
108. Quoted in Chapman, *The Pony Express*, p. 229.
109. Quoted in Driggs, *The Pony Express Goes Through*, p. 180.
110. Burton, *The City of the Saints*, p. 176.
111. Quoted in Richard Dunlop, *Great Trails of the West*. Nashville, TN: Abingdon Press, 1971, p. 246.
112. Quoted in Driggs, *The Pony Express Goes Through*, p. 177.
113. Quoted in Driggs, *The Pony Express Goes Through*, pp. 147–48.
114. Quoted in Driggs, *The Pony Express Goes Through*, pp. 148–49.
115. Quoted in Driggs, *The Pony Express Goes Through*, p. 150.
116. Quoted in Chapman, *The Pony Express*, pp. 230–31.
117. Quoted in Visscher, *A Thrilling and Truthful History*, p. 42.
118. Visscher, *A Thrilling and Truthful History*, p. 34.
119. Chapman, *The Pony Express*, p. 275.
120. Quoted in Visscher, *A Thrilling and Truthful History*, p. 62.
121. Quoted in Visscher, *A Thrilling and Truthful History*, p. 59.
122. Bloss, *Pony Express*, p. 63

Chapter 6: The Paiute War

123. Quoted in Driggs, *The Pony Express*

Goes Through, pp. 106–7.

124. Quoted in Bloss, *Pony Express*, p. 64.

125. Quoted in Chapman, *The Pony Express*, p. 232.

126. Quoted in Driggs, *The Pony Express Goes Through*, p. 76.

127. Quoted in Driggs, *The Pony Express Goes Through*, p. 126.

128. Quoted in Driggs, *The Pony Express Goes Through*, pp. 111–12.

129. Quoted in Driggs, *The Pony Express Goes Through*, p. 73.

130. William F. Cody, *Buffalo Bill's Life Story; An Autobiography*. New York: Rinehart & Co., 1920, pp. 47–48.

131. Quoted in Visscher, *A Thrilling and Truthful History*, p. 45.

132. Quoted in Visscher, *A Thrilling and Truthful History*, p. 45.

133. Quoted in Bloss, *Pony Express*, p. 74.

134. Quoted in Driggs, *The Pony Express Goes Through*, p. 78.

135. Bloss, *Pony Express*, p. 98.

136. Nevin, *The Expressmen*, p. 88.

Epilogue: "Farewell, Pony!"

137. Driggs, *The Pony Express Goes Through*, p. 49.

138. Quoted in Driggs, *The Pony Express Goes Through*, pp. 57–58.

139. Quoted in Summerfield, *U.S. Mail*, p. 73.

140. Quoted in Driggs, *The Pony Express Goes Through*, p. 166.

141. Visscher, *A Thrilling and Truthful History*, p. 48.

142. Settle, *Saddles and Spurs*, p. 211.

For Further Reading

Joe Benson, *The Traveler's Guide to the Pony Express Trail*. Helena, MT: Falcon Publishing, 1995. Traces the Pony Express trail with descriptions of each section. Includes maps and photos. Useful for planning an entertaining and educational vacation.

William F. Cody, *Buffalo Bill's Life Story: An Autobiography*. New York: Rinehart & Co., 1920. The story of William Cody's life including the period he served as a Pony Express rider.

Lee Jensen, *The Pony Express*. New York: Grosset & Dunlap, 1955. Dated but entertaining account of the Pony Express including background, details of the first ride, trouble with Native Americans, and adventures experienced by some of the riders. Illustrated with original and period drawings and a map showing the route of the Pony Express.

Fred Reinfeld, *Pony Express*. New York: Macmillan, 1966. Complete, well-written, and easy-to-read account of the Pony Express saga. Recommended reading.

Mark Twain, *Roughing It*. 1871. Reprint, New York: Harper & Brothers, 1959. The author's personal narrative of his experiences as a young man in the West in the early 1860s. Includes a chapter on the Pony Express.

Tom West, *Heroes on Horseback: The Story of the Pony Express*. New York: Four Winds Press, 1969. Dramatized but fact-filled account of the Pony Express, illustrated by period photos.

Works Consulted

Books

Roy S. Bloss, *Pony Express—The Great Gamble*. Berkeley, CA: Howell-North Press, 1959. An excellent resource that includes the findings and analyses of the author's search through historical material. Includes appendices of Pony Express riders and stations by state.

Richard F. Burton, *The City of the Saints and Across the Rocky Mountains to California*. 1862. Reprint, Niwot: University Press of Colorado, 1990. A factual account of the American West written by an English observer who crossed the country by stagecoach just prior to the Civil War.

Arthur Chapman, *The Pony Express: The Record of a Romantic Adventure in Business*. 1932. Reprint, New York: Cooper Square Publishers, 1971. Well-written and fact-filled history of the Pony Express that includes riders' quotes and excerpts from newspapers and periodicals of the time.

Everett Dick, *Vanguards of the Frontier*. New York: D. Appleton-Century, 1941. Includes a brief early account of the Pony Express venture.

Howard R. Driggs, *The Pony Express Goes Through: An American Saga Told by Its Heroes*. New York: J. B. Lippincott, 1935. Colorful and easy-to-read account of the Pony Express. Includes conversations with Pony riders who were interviewed by the author later in their lives.

Richard Dunlop, *Great Trails of the West*. Nashville, TN: Abingdon Press, 1971. Contains a chapter that describes some stations along the Pony Express trail as they were in 1971, along with snippets of history about the Pony Express.

Anthony Godfrey, *Historic Resource Study: Pony Express National Historic Trail*. United States Department of the Interior/National Park Service, 1994. Review of the Pony Express adventure with emphasis on the history, location, and operation of stations along the historic route.

Horace Greeley, *An Overland Journey from New York to San Francisco in the Summer of 1859*, 1860. Reprint, New York: Knopf, 1964. First-person account of *New York Tribune* editor Horace Greeley's journey from New York to San Francisco by stage in the summer of 1859.

LeRoy Hafen, *The Overland Mail, 1849–1869*. Cleveland: Arthur H. Clark, 1926. The history of overland mail service at a pivotal point in U.S. history. Includes a chapter on the Pony Express with emphasis on the first ride and business aspects of the venture.

Alexander Majors, *Seventy Years On the Frontier*. 1893. Reprint, Minneapolis: Ross & Haines, 1965. The memoirs of freight man Alexander Majors, one of the key members of Russell, Majors & Waddell and backer of the Pony Express.

James Monaghan, *The Overland Trail*. Indianapolis: Bobbs-Merrill, 1947. History of the exploration and development of overland routes across North America beginning with Lewis and Clark and concluding with the transcontinental railroad. Contains a chapter on the Pony Express.

David Nevin, *The Expressmen*. New York: Time-Life Books, 1974. Contains an informative chapter on the Pony Express, complete with color illustrations and period photographs of the men and locales that were a part of the great adventure.

Arthur King Peters, *Seven Trails West*. New York: Abbeville Press, 1996. Explores major land routes that linked east with west in the United States including the Lewis and Clark Trail, the Oregon–California Trail, and the route of the transcontinental telegraph and railroad. Contains a chapter on the Pony Express, complete with period and color photos.

Frank A. Root and William Elsey Connelley, *The Overland Stage to California*. Topeka, KS: W. Y. Morgan, 1901. A history of the Overland Stage, including a chapter on the Pony Express. The author Frank Root was an express messenger who rode the Overland Stage beginning in 1863.

Bruce A. Rosenberg, *The Code of the West*. Bloomington: Indiana University Press, 1982. The author explores several famous episodes in western history including Custer's Last Stand, the California gold rush, and the Pony Express. He investigates the enduring popularity of such episodes and their meaning for Americans today.

Raymond W. and Mary Lund Settle, *Saddles and Spurs: The Pony Express Saga*. Lincoln: University of Nebraska Press, 1955. One of the most definitive and complete works on the Pony Express. Includes background on the overland mail issue, details on the setup and organization of the Pony Express, biographical sketches of the riders, descriptions of the stations, and an overview of the Paiute War.

———, *War Drums and Wagon Wheels: The Story of Russell, Majors and Waddell*. Lincoln: University of Nebraska Press, 1966. A history of transportation on the Great Plains in the mid–nineteenth century, with emphasis on the rise and fall of the freighting firm of Russell, Majors & Waddell.

Arthur E. Summerfield, *U.S. Mail: The Story of the United States Postal Service*. New York: Holt, Rinehart and Winston, 1960. Contains a summary of the Pony Express as a proud chapter of U.S. Postal Service history.

William Lightfoot Visscher, *A Thrilling and Truthful History of the Pony Express or Blazing the Westward Way*. Chicago: Charles T. Powner, 1946. Interesting account of the Pony Express that includes a chapter on "Pony Bob" Haslam, whom the author interviewed. The author's style is wordy and outdated, and the second half of the work wanders from the Pony Express story, but the book is informative and worthwhile nevertheless.

Periodicals

"Danger of an Interruption in the Pony Express," *San Francisco Daily Evening Bulletin*, May 26, 1860. An Indian uprising in the summer of 1860 threatens the future of the Pony Express. The article includes agent W. W. Finney's efforts to secure protection for at-risk riders and station attendants.

"Pony Express. Nine Days from San Francisco to New York," *San Francisco Daily Evening Bulletin*, March 17, 1860. One of the first announcements of the Pony Express to be published in a Western newspaper.

Martin Ridge, "Reflections on the Pony Express," *Montana: The Magazine of Western History*, Autumn 1996. Well-written article looking back on the Pony Express as a part of the nation's heritage. Includes an overview of the enterprise, a map of the route, and period photos.

Index

Picture Credits

About the Author

Diane Yancey works as a freelance writer in the Pacific Northwest, where she has lived for over twenty years. She writes nonfiction for middle-grade and high school readers and enjoys traveling and collecting old books. Some of her other books relating to U.S. history in the 1800s include *Camels for Uncle Sam*, *Civil War Generals of the Union*, *Leaders of the Civil War*, *Strategic Battles of the Civil War*, and *Desperadoes and Dynamite: Train Robbery in the United States*.